8,3/4.0

Rediscovering Easter Island

Rediscovering Easter Island

HOW HISTORY IS INVENTED

Kathy Pelta

LERNER PUBLICATIONS COMPANY
MINNEAPOLIS

For their help, thanks to Linda Oliver and the staff of the Curtis Memorial Library in Brunswick, Maine, and to Grant McCall. A special thanks also to my sister Marjorie Birdsall of Santiago, Chile; to my brother-in-law Jose Nuñez, who was navigator on the first flight from Chile to Easter Island in 1951; and to Arne Skjølsvold of Oslo, Norway, who was with the Norwegian Archaeological Expedition to Easter Island in 1955–1956 and on later expeditions as well.

Lerner Publications Company
A division of Lerner Publishing Group
241 First Avenue North
Minneapolis, MN 55401 U.S.A.

Website address: www.lernerbooks.com

Library of Congress Cataloging-in-Publication Data

Pelta, Kathy.
    Rediscovering Easter Island / by Kathy Pelta.
    p.   cm. — (How history is invented)
    Includes bibliographical references and index.
    Summary: Discusses the many visits made by explorers, missionaries, businesspeople, scientists, and others to Easter Island since the late 1600s and what they revealed about life on this remote Pacific island.
    ISBN 0-8225-4890-9 (lib. bdg. : alk. paper)
    1. Easter Island—History—Juvenile literature. 2. Easter Island—Antiquities—Juvenile literature. [1. Easter Island.]
I. Title. II. Series.
F3169 .P45 2001
996.1'8—dc21   00-009163

Manufactured in the United States of America
1 2 3 4 5 6 – A – 06 05 04 03 02 01

CONTENTS
—❧ ‡ ☙—

Easter Island has few sandy beaches along its rocky shorelines, and only one is suitable for landing canoes.

INTRODUCTION

ON A MAP, EASTER ISLAND LOOKS LIKE A TINY DOT in the middle of the vast Pacific Ocean. But in the minds of many people, it is a huge question mark. The island is shrouded in mystery—prompting more questions than answers. What is the meaning of the brooding stone figures *(moai)* that crowd the tiny island? Why are they so large—some as tall as telephone poles and as heavy as three or four automobiles?

And what of the ancient people who carved the somber-faced gray statues? Where did they live before they settled on the island they called Rapa Nui? And how—without machines, draft animals, or even wheels—did they move these towering giants from the rock quarry where they were carved to their final locations miles away? According to local legend, the statues walked! No wonder many people have called Easter Island the "island of mystery."

Easter Island is shaped like a triangle, with an inactive volcano on each corner. It has few sandy beaches along the thirty-five mile rocky coastline, and only one is suitable for landing canoes. The island covers an area of sixty-four square miles, scarcely more than twice the size of the island of Manhattan. Easter Island—still called Rapa Nui by its people—is the most remote inhabited island in the world. The nearest neighbor to the east is Chile, some twenty-three hundred

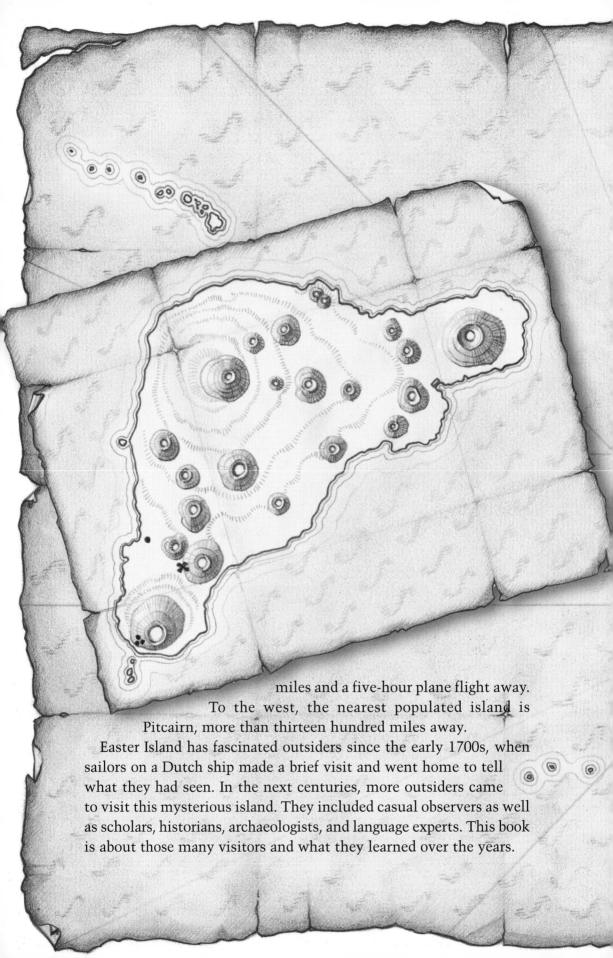

miles and a five-hour plane flight away.
To the west, the nearest populated island is
Pitcairn, more than thirteen hundred miles away.
Easter Island has fascinated outsiders since the early 1700s, when
sailors on a Dutch ship made a brief visit and went home to tell
what they had seen. In the next centuries, more outsiders came
to visit this mysterious island. They included casual observers as well
as scholars, historians, archaeologists, and language experts. This book
is about those many visitors and what they learned over the years.

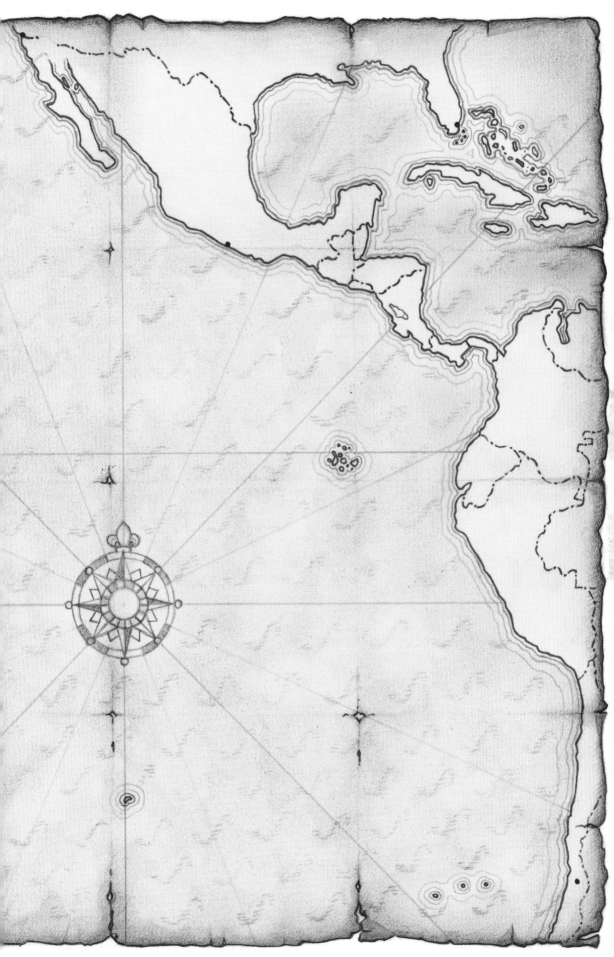

Early visitors to Easter Island may have arrived in large oceangoing canoes, which may have had sails.

—— ❧ ONE ❧ ——

THE FIRST VISITORS

1722–1771

THE STORY OF EASTER ISLAND'S "DISCOVERY" BEGINS in the late 1600s, some thirty years before an outsider actually set foot on the island. Spain was the richest country in Europe. Its empire reached from the Spanish Netherlands (modern-day Belgium) to vast areas of North and South America. The viceroyalty of Peru was the center of Spanish power in South America, and from this seaport Spanish ships were sailing home, their holds filled with New World gold. Scouting the same waters were buccaneers, or pirates from many parts of Europe, waiting to attack the treasure-laden Spanish galleons.

One such buccaneer was the Englishman Edward Davis. In the 1680s, while sailing in the South Pacific in search of ships to plunder, Davis reported seeing a low and sandy island. Farther to the west, he saw some hills. He calculated their location to be about five hundred leagues, or fifteen hundred miles, west of Chile—then a province of Peru. Davis later told English buccaneer William Dampier about the island he had seen and the range of hills just beyond.

At that time, no one knew much about the South Seas, and the land that Davis described interested Dampier. Could this be the huge landmass that geographers thought should be somewhere in theSouth Pacific Ocean?

Buccaneer William Dampier

In 1697 William Dampier wrote a book about his travels, *A New Voyage Around the World.* In it, he described the Davis voyage— mentioning the island Edward Davis had spotted and the hills beyond. And Dampier repeated Davis's suspicion that those hills might be part of a southern continent.

Two years later, Lionel Wafer, the surgeon's mate on Davis's ship, also wrote a book describing the lands Davis had seen. Wafer's book, *A New Voyage and Description of the Isthmus of America . . . with remarkable occurrences in the South Seas and elsewhere,* was published in England in 1699. The following year, a publisher in Holland printed a Dutch translation.

The Dutch Give the Island a Name

In Holland the news about Davis's sightings delighted the directors of the Dutch West India Trading Company. Although the trading company had outposts on the African coast and along the Hudson River in North America, it was not as prosperous as its rival in the East Indies, the Dutch East India Trading Company. The directors of the Dutch West India Trading Company saw this chance to expand their trade. They mistakenly thought the land might be part of a huge new continent.

The company outfitted three small ships, put Dutch sea captain Jacob Roggeveen in charge, and sent him to the South Pacific to investigate. With 223 crewmen, food to last two years, and the three ships equipped with cannons, Roggeveen set sail from Holland on July 16, 1721, bound for the coast of Chile. From there he sailed due west, according to Davis's directions.

At that time, navigators could find latitude (distance north or south of the equator) fairly accurately. But finding exact longitude (distance east or west of a standard point, such as Greenwich or Paris) was more difficult. This measurement depended on an accurate knowledge of time, and navigators had no reliable timekeepers.

Roggeveen continued as far as Davis had calculated the distance to be. When he did not find the flat and sandy island Davis had described—and the hoped-for southern continent just beyond—he sailed west about two hundred leagues (some six hundred miles) more.

The Dutch East India Trading Company building in Amsterdam, Holland. This trading company was founded in 1602.

The Legend: The Ariki Mau Finds a Home

Islanders told and retold the story of the island and sometimes embellished it to please the listener. Eventually there were many versions, including the one below. In one version of the legend, the supreme chief's tattooer, Haumaka, had a vision of a new and pleasant land where Hotu Matu`a should go. In still other versions, before departing Hotu Matu`a sent six men ahead in a canoe to look for a fine beach where he could settle. Another legend tells how the king chose six men, gave them a canoe, and told them to sail straight ahead until they reached the land Haumaka's soul had seen, with a beach worthy of a supreme chief. One feature that seems to be common to all versions is that the first settlers came from a far-off island, probably to the west, about nine hundred years before the first European visitors arrived in 1722.

No one knows if the first settlers reached Rapa Nui by chance, or if their navigator already knew the way. Whether the discovery was accidental or by design, the early Polynesians (people indigenous to the islands in the south and west Pacific Ocean) were extremely skilled sailors and often made long sea voyages. To find their way by day, they studied the winds and the position of the sun, the motion of the waves, and the movements of seabirds. On clear nights, they let the stars be their guides.

Long ago, Hotu Matu`a, ariki mau [supreme chief] of his clan, left his home on the island called Hiva [a far-off place] to find a new home. Hotu Matu`a had been forced to leave Hiva when his clan was defeated in battle. The departure was sudden.

Hotu Matu`a sailed in a great double-hulled canoe with family, friends, servants, his maste builder, and men wise in the art of rongorongo [the writing and reading of hieroglyphic symbols]. In the new land, these masters would teach young students to read and inscribe rongorongo tablets. Sixty-seven of these sacred tablets were stowed in the canoe, along with food for the journey and sprouts, seedlings, and tree roots the people would need to start gardens and orchards when they reached their new home.

After a journey of 120 days, the great canoe reached a small island with a rocky coast. The travelers circled around the island until they found a sandy beach. Here the water was calm enough to beach the canoe. At the moment of landing, Hotu Matu`a's wife gave birth.

Hotu Matu`a, his wife, and their new baby boy lived in a cave called ana kena [cave of the kena bird] while the master builder constructed a fine stone house fit for the king, and another beside it for the queen and baby. Nearby he built an outdoor kitchen with a five-sided earth oven. From the house of Hotu Matu`a, a broad stone path led down to the sandy shore—which only the supreme chief, his family, and their servants were allowed to use. Here, at the bay of Anakena, the king stayed apart from his people. His family grew to include several sons.

The other new arrivals explored the island to find places to settle. To clear land for planting, they cut down and burned trees. They used the ash to fertilize their gardens. At first the people had only wild ferns and sandalwood nuts to eat, along with birds and birds' eggs, turtles from the beach, and sea urchins and eels they found in the tide pools. But soon the gardens gave them taros [a starchy tuber], yams, sugarcane, and bananas as well as the paper mulberry tree, whose bark was used to make cloth.

The supreme chief visited his people many times. He joined in their feasts and festivals and taught them chants. In time, Hotu Matu`a grew old. When he was about to die, he called his sons to his side. To the eldest he gave the title of ariki mau and the land around the bay of Anakena. To his other sons he gave other parts of the island.

And so the island was divided, and a certain family, or clan, lived in each part. Many years passed. At the statue-building time, every clan built its own ahu [religious altar]. Whenever the chief of a clan died, his people carved moai [huge statues] to capture the chief's mana [supernatural powers]. In this way, the mana that had once been in the head of a chief was transferred to the head of the statue and would not be lost. The chief's mana would bring good luck to the people of the village. Rain would fall, crop would thrive, chickens would lay many eggs, the fishers would catch many fish, and the people would have many babies.

Then on April 2, 1722, the Dutch commander saw a turtle, floating weeds, and birds—signs that land was near. Later that day, someone spotted what looked like a sandy island. A cheer went up. If this was the island Davis had spotted thirty-five years earlier, then just beyond would be the new southern continent.

Before sailing on, Roggeveen decided to explore the small island. He had seen smoke rising, so he felt sure it was inhabited. This would give him a chance to barter for fruit and other food. Because it was Easter Sunday, the men named their discovery *Paasch Eyland*, Dutch for Easter Island.

When the Dutch fleet was only two miles from shore, a curious and cheerful islander paddled out to one of the ships in a canoe. After crewmen helped him aboard, the man skittered about the deck. With great interest, he examined all parts of the vessel. He ran his hands over the mast, the sails, the booms, the ropes, and the guns. When he saw his face reflected in a mirror, he jumped back, startled, and then peeked behind the glass to see who was there. Soon he departed in his canoe with gifts from the crew—a small mirror, a pair of scissors, and two strings of blue glass beads that he had hung around his neck.

As the Dutch flotilla moved nearer to shore to drop anchor, the crewmen saw on the island great numbers of what appeared to be huge stone idols. With a closer look, Roggeveen was shocked to realize that what he had taken for sand was scorched hay or grass. So this was not the sandy island Davis had seen after all—which meant no new continent lay just beyond. In his ship's log, Roggeveen wrote that if this was not Davis Island, then Edward Davis and his crew "must stand convicted of a whole bunch of lies in their reports." Apparently it did not occur to the Dutch captain that Davis might also have mistaken dry, withered vegetation for sand.

The next day, more islanders, swimming and in canoes, came to greet the Dutch ships. They did not wait to receive gifts. Instead, they grabbed what they could, then dove into the water and headed for shore. They seemed especially fond of caps and hats, which they boldly snatched from the seamen's heads.

Some of Easter Island's statues, the moai, seem randomly placed along the hillsides. Over time, dirt and rubble have buried all but their heads.

The following morning, Dutch sailors armed with muskets went ashore to explore. As they tried to march in formation, islanders crowded in to block their way. A scuffle began as some islanders grabbed for the sailors' jackets and weapons. Shots rang out. When the skirmish was over, a dozen islanders lay dead.

After that, there was no more gunfire. One islander seemed to give directions to the others, who left and soon returned with food. Gesturing with their hands, the Dutch indicated they did not want the sugarcane or yams, but they happily accepted sixty chickens and thirty bunches of bananas. In payment they presented colorful, striped cloth to the islanders, who seemed pleased with the trade.

The Dutch visitors continued their tour. They were greatly impressed with the tall, carved statues they had spotted from the ship when they first arrived. Both Roggeveen and his officer, a German named Carl Behrens, kept notes during their visit. Roggeveen used his ship's log to make long, detailed entries. Although Behrens noted the island was "full of woods and forests," Roggeveen said he saw no large trees. He commented that many statues were nearly thirty feet high, and he could not understand how the people were able to erect such huge figures without trees and without hemp to make strong ropes. He decided that the statues were not carved from stone and moved there from someplace else but instead were made of clay on the spot.

The Dutch saw nothing made of metal on the island and no domestic animals except chickens. They found the people tall, with well-proportioned limbs, strong muscles, and snow-white teeth. Some of the people wore cloaks made from strips of bark or plant fiber that had been sewn together. What amazed the Dutch most about the people's appearance were their long earlobes. The visitors concluded that the lobes had been pierced or slit when the islanders were young, and then round or oval ornaments had been inserted. Eventually, the size and weight of the ornaments—often pieces of a vegetable root such as parsnip—stretched the earlobes until they reached the person's shoulders.

The canoes the Dutch visitors saw on the island were made of small boards laced together with fine twine. The people had no caulking to make the seams tight, so these canoes leaked badly. When the islanders took the canoes into the ocean, they appeared to spend most of their time bailing out seawater.

A typical island house was about fifty feet long by fifteen feet wide. Rushes or long grass tied to wood frames formed the walls and roof. The people cooked in earth ovens. They dug a hole in the ground, lined it with pebbles, and then built a fire with dry grass. To cook, they wrapped their food in damp swamp grasses and set it in the fire.

An islander—possibly a chief—invited the Dutch to see the banana plantations and fruit trees on the other side of the island. The visitors declined. A wind was coming up, and it seemed wiser for them to set sail at once. Although the Dutch did not stay long and did not completely explore Easter Island, Roggeveen's detailed log and Behrens's notes provided the only descriptions of the island before its people had additional contact with foreigners.

After leaving Easter Island, the Dutch fleet sailed westward, still searching for the sandy island that Davis had seen. They found neither the island nor the presumed southern continent. After a storm destroyed one Dutch ship, the other two battered vessels limped on to Batavia.

Batavia (a port later known as Jakarta, capital of Indonesia) was headquarters for the Dutch East India Trading Company. So when the two vessels of the Dutch West India Trading Company arrived, officials charged the commander with trespassing. They confiscated his two ships, arrested everyone aboard, including Roggeveen, and sent them back to Holland. Although Dutch law courts later dropped the charges against Roggeveen, he never again saw his ship's log, which Dutch East India Trading Company officials had seized along with other records and the two ships.

In 1728 an unknown seaman on the voyage published a sometimes fanciful report of the Dutch adventure, in which he told of meeting islanders twelve feet tall. Nine years later, Behrens published his less sensational version of events, which was later reprinted in several German and French travel books.

Spain Claims a New Colony

For the next fifty years, Easter Islanders saw no more outsiders, even though explorers still searched the South Pacific for the so-called Davis Island and the elusive southern continent just beyond. Since most ships sailing the South Pacific called at Batavia for repairs, provisions, and fresh water, there were plenty of sailors to trade sea yarns and spread rumors about the latest South Seas discoveries. According to one rumor, Davis Island and the island Roggeveen had visited were one and the same.

Tattooing and Other Decorative Practices on Easter Island

Islanders liked to decorate their bodies with tattoos. Often they had their thighs and lower legs tattooed in a way that made it seem as though they were wearing stockings or pants. Some of the older chiefs had tattoos that covered much of their bodies—even their lips.

Tattooing was often done when a person was very young—eight or nine years old. The tattooist used a sharp piece of fish or bird bone carved in the shape of a tooth, with three or four tiny points at the end. He dipped this "needle" into a mixture of charcoal and juice from a native plant. When the bone was in position, the tattoo artist hit the bone with a small wooden stick to puncture the flesh. The tattoo could be a geometric design or pictures of birds or plants. One islander had a tattoo showing British sailors carrying off a religious icon.

Sometimes islanders enhanced tattoos by painting their bodies with red, white, or gray clay. Some islanders also stretched their earlobes. Soon after the arrival of missionaries (members of a religious group who seek to convert others to their faith) in the 1860s, the islanders abandoned both tattooing and the custom of stretching their earlobes.

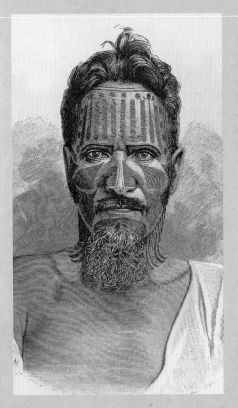

A geometric tattoo design covers this Rapanui man's face.

Meanwhile, Spain's empire was shrinking. Spain and France had lost North American land and people to Great Britain. Great Britain was becoming a serious threat to Spain. It ruled the seas with a strong navy and outposts around the world. Ever since the days of the buccaneers, British ships had continued to sail the waters around South America. Then, in 1765, British warships occupied Islas Malvinas (Falkland Islands) in the Atlantic Ocean, off South America's east coast. The action worried Spain's King Carlos (Charles) III. Even though Spain ruled all of South America—except for Brazil, a Portuguese colony—the king was uneasy about Great Britain's intentions. He feared Great Britain would build a naval base at some island in the Pacific Ocean, off South America's west coast, as well.

With the king's blessings, the viceroy (king's governor) of Peru took action. He knew about the island Davis had sighted, and he had probably read Behrens's account of the Dutch voyage to Easter Island. In 1770 the viceroy sent Don Felipe González y Haedo to the same area with orders to seize this island—whether it was Davis Island or Easter Island—before the British could claim it.

González outfitted two warships, *San Lorenzo* and *Rosalía,* and set off on his mission, sailing from the Peruvian port of Callao, near Lima, early in October. Five weeks later, he arrived at Easter Island, which he called Davis Island. At the start of the Spaniards' six-day stay, González drew a map of the island, naming coves and points of land and taking soundings (measuring water depths).

Much as their grandparents had met the Dutch fifty years earlier, islanders swam and paddled out to the ships in outrigger canoes to greet the new arrivals. The people clambered on deck, then raced about investigating. They climbed the rigging and even danced while Spanish sailors played bagpipes and fifes.

When the Spaniards went ashore, an officer ordered that any man who did not pay for gifts with items worth even more would be severely flogged. So in return for the islanders' gifts of bananas, chili peppers, sweet potatoes, and chickens, crewmen presented the people with ribbons, trinkets, parts of navy uniforms, hats, small gilt-metal crosses, and in one case, a plateful of salt pork and cooked rice to eat.

On their brief tour of the island, González and his men observed the islanders' thatch-covered houses, their vegetable gardens, banana groves, and sugarcane fields. They saw few birds except seagulls and no thick stands of timber. They reported seeing only two small outrigger canoes on the whole island. Like the Dutch, these later visitors guessed that the cloaks some islanders wore were made by sewing together fibers from stems of a plant—possibly banana. And like the Dutch, the Spaniards stood in awe of the immense statues. They wondered how these giants had been erected and what kept them from falling down. Unlike the Dutch, who believed the statues had been made of clay, a Spaniard struck a statue with a metal hoe and made a spark—proving the material was hard rock.

On the last day of their stay, the Spanish visitors held a ceremony to officially claim the island for their king. With flags flying and drums beating, 250 sailors and officers and two priests marched to the eastern end of the island. Some 800 curious islanders joined in, singing and dancing along with the moving procession as they shouted, *"Makemake"*—an expression the Spanish did not understand.

Atop three hillocks (small hills), men erected three large crosses. The priests chanted litanies, with both the Spaniards and enthusiastic islanders repeating the Latin responses. An officer then proclaimed the island's name to be Isla de San Carlos (San Carlos Island) and declared King Carlos III to be the islanders' lawful sovereign. He gave the chiefs of the island a paper to sign to indicate they were satisfied. A few islanders obliged by scratching marks on the paper. One drew a bird. Following a twenty-one-gun salute from the ships, everyone shouted, *"Viva el Rey"* (long live the king). Then the Spaniards departed.

González arrived back in Callao in late December 1770. The following February he sent his official report, along with the ship's log, to the Peruvian viceroy in Lima. By early spring, details of the voyage were common knowledge in Peruvian and Chilean ports. Before long, letters mailed from those towns carried news about the Spanish adventures to Great Britain and other parts of Europe. By December 1771, accounts of the Spanish voyage appeared in London

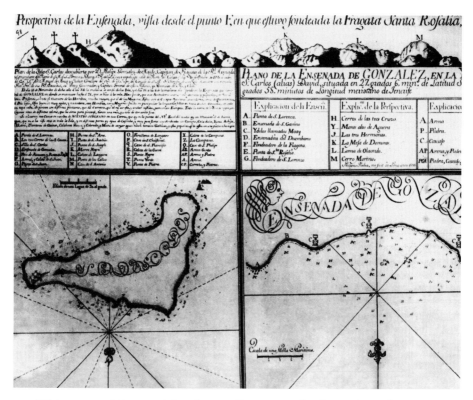

This map of Easter Island was drawn in the late 1700s by Spanish explorers, who named the island Isla de San Carlos.

newspapers. A typical report was one in a London newspaper, *Lloyd's Evening Post and British Chronicle,* in its December 2, 1771, issue. The article stated that the inhabitants of the island "jumped into the water and swam to meet the ships, offering fruits, poultry, etc. and even their cloaths [clothes] which are very ordinary and seem to be formed of the herbs and fruits of the country . . . . [T]heir disposition is perfectly mild . . . . [A] fertile soil, which leaves nothing for the inhabitants to wish for, softens their manners and inclines them to humanity . . . . [T]hey live in caves and grottoes [cavelike structures] under ground and worship stone statues of a gigantic size."

—❧ TWO ❧—

SPREADING THE WORD

1774–1797

I N JULY 1772, EXPLORER JAMES COOK SET SAIL FROM Plymouth, England, with two ships, *Resolution* and *Adventure,* on his second voyage to the South Pacific. By then scientists no longer believed there was a huge undiscovered land mass to the south (Australia had been discovered much earlier). Even so, Cook's orders were to search the area and prove "once [and] for all" that none existed. For nearly two years, Captain Cook zigzagged across the South Pacific. He crossed the Antarctic Circle and probably sailed closer to the South Pole than anyone before, but as he expected, he did not find the so-called "southern continent." Finally, in desperate need of fresh water and provisions, he headed to Easter Island.

James Cook knew about the voyage of Davis in the 1680s from reading Lionel Wafer's book, and he was familiar with Carl Behrens's account of Roggeveen's 1722 voyage to Easter Island. Before leaving England, Cook had also learned that a Spanish ship had recently sailed to the island. By that time, people assumed that Davis's Land

After crossing the South Pacific Ocean to explore the unchartered waters, James Cook (opposite) landed at Easter Island.

and Easter Island were one and the same. None but the Spanish ever called it San Carlos Island.

Captain Cook arrived at Easter Island's Hanga Roa Bay on March 1, 1774, four years after the Spanish visit. Traveling with Cook were the German natural history experts Johann Forster and his son George.

When men from the ship went ashore, a swarm of islanders met them. The British crew handed out pieces of cloth, nails, mirrors, and other trinkets, then made signs that they wanted food. Soon the people brought them bananas, potatoes, and sugarcane.

Since Cook had been ill and was feeling too weak to walk far, he sent a small group—including the Forsters—to explore the island. Meanwhile he and a few others from the ship stayed closer to the landing place. They studied details of two or three giant statues that stood nearby, and then they wandered along the shore to observe the islanders. One of Cook's men drew sketches. From the attire of some islanders, the British saw evidence of the Spanish visit four years earlier. One islander wore a broad-brimmed European hat. Another sported a wool coat, and a third had a bright red silk handkerchief. A Tahitian man with the Cook expedition spoke with the islanders in a Tahitian dialect that they seemed to understand.

In the evening, the Forsters returned to tell of their day's adventures. They said that when they began their walk, islanders had crowded around them. Then a middle-aged man—with his face painted white and his body "punctured from head to foot" (tattooed)—suddenly appeared. He carried a spear on which he hung a piece of white cloth. This seemed to be a peace sign, for the crowd drew back to let the man lead the visitors while they followed at a respectful distance.

The two naturalists said they saw few birds, no animals except chickens and rats, and no trees. Their search for fresh water was not too successful. All the water they found—even the water used by the islanders—was either harsh-tasting, salty, or dirty. Johann and George Forster also described a number of huge statues they had seen. Some were standing, with large cylinder-shaped stones on their heads.

These restored moai at Anakena Beach may be the same ones that Cook's crew described when they returned to their ship.

Others had fallen to the ground. Cook and the Forsters discussed ways the early islanders might have raised the huge figures and then placed the heavy stones on their heads.

Captain Cook later estimated that about six hundred people lived on the island. To him, they seemed shorter and thinner than those Behrens had described in his account of the Roggeveen expedition. But like the Dutch, these British visitors and the German naturalists found the islanders pleasant, though "much addicted to pilfering." Every chance they had, the people tried to take the British sailors' hats.

In 1777 Cook published a book about his first two voyages to the South Pacific—including his three days on Easter Island. Captain Cook told of seeing only three or four small canoes on Easter Island. He said they were made from planks of wood sewn together and were not seaworthy. The islanders had neither the materials nor the knowledge to caulk the cracks, he thought. Cook also noted that parts of the island had plantations producing sugarcane, sweet potatoes, and bananas, while other parts of the island looked as if they had once been under cultivation but no longer were. The same year Cook released his book, George Forster also published a book about the expedition. Forster reported that he did not see a single tree more than ten feet tall on the island.

Although Cook concluded Easter Island was a poor choice for a port of call—without safe anchorage, wood for fuel, or fresh water worth taking on board—his book fascinated readers with its descriptions of the giant statues and brought lasting fame to Easter Island. Wooden carvings from Easter Island, either acquired as gifts or in trade, were brought back to London by members of Cook's expedition and later displayed at the British Museum. They included a delicate carving of a human hand and a *rapa*—a wooden paddle used in certain dances. For the first time, the people of London had a chance to view Easter Island artifacts.

La Pérouse's Busy Day

In the late summer of 1785, France's King Louis XVI sent explorer Jean-François de Galaup, Comte de La Pérouse on a three-year cruise around the world to discover new lands and investigate lands recently discovered. Commanding two warships, La Pérouse sailed to Easter Island, following both Spanish charts and Cook's sailing directions.

The French ships anchored at the island's Hanga Roa Bay in April 1786. On shore, four or five hundred islanders waited to greet this latest round of visitors. The size of the crowd had nearly doubled by the time the French came ashore and pitched the tent that was to be their headquarters for the day.

To La Pérouse, these people did not appear as miserable as those Captain Cook had described in his book. La Pérouse gave them presents, including hogs, goats, and a sheep. Despite the gifts, the islanders seemed as eager as ever to steal whatever they could lay their hands on. Most of all, they seemed to covet handkerchiefs and hats.

Jean-François de Galaup, Comte de La Pérouse

To avoid trouble, La Pérouse promised his soldiers and sailors that he would replace any hats or handkerchiefs that were taken.

La Pérouse had allowed only one day to learn all he could about the island. To save time, he sent out two groups to explore. His group stayed close to the coast. They studied people's houses and also the huge statues—many of which had been toppled. La Pérouse visited one hut that was three hundred feet long and "housed two hundred people." Some of the French took careful measurements of statues and several buildings while a team of artists made drawings to scale.

The French king's royal gardener was with the group that headed inland to examine farming methods. He had brought seeds to start gardens and orchards for the islanders. As he planted the seeds, the gardener tried to explain to the islanders which seeds would become cabbages, carrots, beets, maize (corn), and pumpkins, and which would produce cotton plants and orange and lemon trees.

La Pérouse estimated that only one-tenth of the island was cultivated. He regretted that there were no rivers, streams, or trees on Easter Island. Without trees the land was fully exposed to the rays of

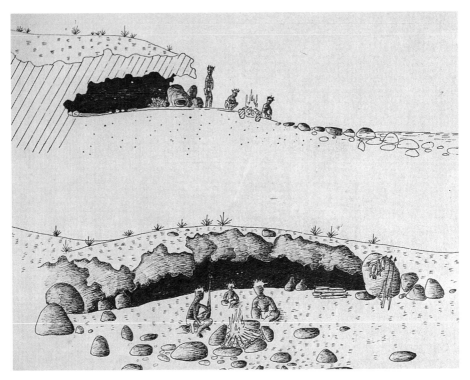

The Padre Sebastian Englert Archaeological Museum on Easter Island displays these drawings of the islanders' early cave homes.

the sun, whereas shade from trees would cool the land. That would cause clouds to condense, he said, and bring to the mountains enough rain to form springs and rivulets. La Pérouse thought cisterns to collect rainwater would be of great help to the islanders.

After his day on Easter Island, the French explorer departed, sure that he had treated the people of Easter Island kindly. During the next year, he visited Alaska, the Hawaiian Islands, the coasts of Japan and Korea, and finally Kamchatka, a peninsula on the northeast coast of Russia. Here La Pérouse turned over his journals, notes, and the artists' sketches to an officer, who then set off with them on a grueling overland journey to France. Although all of his papers made it back home, La Pérouse did not. In 1788 his fleet mysteriously disappeared.

Sketches by the French artists were later turned into engravings to illustrate a 1797 book on La Pérouse's expedition to Easter Island. In his papers, La Pérouse described his disappointment when the islanders robbed the visitors "of everything which it was possible for them to take." He found this especially distressing, since he felt he had made every effort to treat the islanders well. "We employed no violence against them," he wrote. "We landed on the island only with an intention to do them service."

The first visits by outsiders must have made an impression on the Easter Islanders; in songs and stories passed on to later generations, these early visits are mentioned. And on a rock on the island is a carving of an early sailing ship, possibly Roggeveen's or Cook's.

THREE

THE WORLD MOVES IN

1805–1864

WHEN LA PÉROUSE VISITED THE EASTER ISLANDERS in 1785, his only wish had been "to do them service." But by the early 1800s, Easter Island had become a convenient stopping place for whaling ships and vessels hauling cargo between South America and Tahiti, an island another twenty-five hundred miles farther west. Not all of these visitors had such noble intentions.

In 1805 the crew of the American schooner *Nancy* captured ten women and twelve men from Easter Island. The captain intended to use them as slave labor for seal hunting in the Juan Fernandez Islands, off the Chilean coast. When the schooner had sailed away from Easter Island for three days, the captain removed the ropes restraining the prisoners. Immediately the freed men jumped from the ship and began swimming toward home. The women tried to join them, but were held back. According to local legend, all of the men were lost except one. He swam more slowly to save his strength and managed to make it all the way to Easter Island.

The crew of a whaler that was anchored offshore from Easter

Restored moai at Ahu Tahai (opposite)

In the 1800s, stone-throwing islanders often drove back visitors who tried to come ashore.

Island kidnapped several young girls. After keeping them aboard ship for several hours, the sailors threw them overboard. Although the girls managed to swim back to safety, a ship's officer fired into the crowd on shore, killing one man, as the whaler sailed away.

Easter Island Viewed from Afar

It is no wonder, then, that the islanders took to greeting with a barrage of stones any visitor who tried to come ashore. This happened to Russian navigator Otto von Kotzebue, who arrived with a scientific expedition in 1816. Although some islanders seemed eager to trade food for the Russians' iron nails, many more seemed determined to drive away the intruders. The Russians could learn about the island only from a distance, observing what they could as the ship circled the island before departing. Otto von Kotzebue saw only two statues standing on the south coast and not a single statue standing on the west coast near Hanga Roa Bay. Some years before, the Russian ship *Neva* was also prevented from landing. It had circled the island for four days, and the crew had counted twenty upright statues as well as many on the ground.

In 1825 islanders armed with clubs, sticks, and rocks drove off a landing party from the British vessel HMS *Blossom*. Its captain, Frederick William Beechey, also had to learn about the island from a distance. During these years, vessels such as the British schooner *Discoverer* in 1831 and the French ship *La Vénus* in 1838 simply anchored offshore to avoid clashes. Often, friendly islanders would then come out to the ships with the usual gifts of food to trade for cloth or other trinkets. According to Admiral Abel Dupetit-Thouars of *La Vénus*, islanders even climbed onto the ship's deck to treat the crew to a display of energetic dancing that involved a lot of hopping on one leg.

A few years later, the sailing ship *Prudence* anchored near the island, and sailors paddled toward shore in a small boat to do some trading. They were met by islanders who tipped over the boat and tried to take the crewmen's clothes—though apparently what the islanders really wanted was the boat. The captain of the *Prudence* reported the incident to a Honolulu newspaper. He said he had noticed other small European-style boats on the island and suspected those might have been obtained the same way.

Several visitors to this part of the Pacific in the early and mid-1800s wrote books or articles about Easter Island after they returned home. J. A. Moerenhout, a Frenchman, was on a ship that anchored off Easter Island on a cruise from Chile to Tahiti in 1827. An islander, six feet tall and with long earlobes, boarded the ship and invited the

One of the dancing islanders aboard the French ship La Vénus *is wearing a sailor's hat.*

sailors to frolic with island women on the seashore. Moerenhout declined the invitation. He chose instead to view the island from the ship. In a book Moerenhout wrote ten years later, he said many sea captains had told him Easter Islanders made "shameful commerce" of their women, and venereal (sexually transmitted) diseases were common among the islanders. Moerenhout also reported that, from the ship, he saw only one upright statue. Scholars were mystified. Why had Easter Islanders destroyed nearly all of these tall figures and the platforms on which they stood?

Around this time, a government worker in Middelburg, Holland, made a surprising discovery. While searching for a document in the files of the old Dutch West India Trading Company, he came across a package marked: "Papers touching the confiscated West Indian ships *Arent* and *Thienhoven* [Roggeveen's ships], dated the 30th of November, 1722." It contained Jacob Roggeveen's journal—missing for over one hundred years! Historians no longer had to depend on exaggerated claims by unknown seamen or on Carl Behrens's sometimes unreliable observations. At last they had an official, detailed record of the first known visit by Europeans to Easter Island.

Peruvian Slave Traders

Some 137 years after the first relatively peaceful meeting between Easter Islanders and outsiders, the situation had changed. By 1859 slave traders had begun capturing Easter Islanders—then numbering about three thousand—and selling them to guano companies in Peru. (Peru was no longer part of the Spanish empire.) Guano, the droppings of seabirds, could be made into a profitable fertilizer. But collecting it along the rocky ledges of Peru's offshore islands was treacherous and extremely unpleasant. Paid workers refused the task, so guano companies sought slaves instead. At first, the Peruvian slavers took only a few people from Easter Island each time.

In the fall of 1862, French naval officer Captain Lejeune of the French vessel *Cassini* stopped at Easter Island. While trading with the friendly islanders, the captain decided the people—and their island— needed someone to protect them. He intended to suggest to French

Roman Catholic missionaries in Chile that they establish a mission on Easter Island. But before he had the chance, disaster struck.

In December 1862, eight slave ships from Peru arrived at Easter Island. This time they made off with about one thousand prisoners. According to accounts by those who managed to escape, armed men came ashore and spread gifts on the beach. As unsuspecting islanders bent to examine the goods, the men grabbed them. The Peruvian slavers shot a dozen islanders who tried to run away and chained the rest in holds of the ships.

Within a few months, most of the islanders taken away had perished from disease and the deplorable working conditions. Fortunately at least one managed to escape and flee to Tahiti, where he told Tepano Jaussen, the Catholic bishop of Tahiti, what had happened. The bishop persuaded the Peruvian government to release the one hundred or so workers still living and send them home. Of these, all but fifteen died of smallpox and tuberculosis on the return trip. The handful who made it back infected their fellow Easter Islanders, setting off a smallpox epidemic that took even more lives.

Those who survived these crushing disasters felt helpless and confused. Besides losing relatives and friends, they no longer had anyone to guide them. This was due to the fact that among the prisoners taken by the slavers was the last supreme chief, Kai Makoi, six of his children, and all of the island's wise men and religious leaders. In the midst of this turmoil, the first missionary arrived, determined to bring the Roman Catholic religion to Easter Island.

───·ᢟ FOUR ᢞ·───

MISSIONARIES AND OTHERS

1864–1872

ASTER ISLAND'S FIRST MISSIONARY WAS EUGÈNE Eyraud. Born in France, Eyraud was a mechanic by trade. As a young man, he worked in South America to support a brother who was studying to be a priest. Once his brother became a missionary, Eyraud decided he also wanted to be a missionary. He discovered he could enter a religious order as a novice— one who does not take the final vows of a priest. So he joined the Fathers of the Holy Spirit in Chile. Then in 1862, as Brother Eugène Eyraud, he sailed with other Roman Catholic missionaries bound for Easter Island, twenty-three hundred miles to the west.

Instead of going directly to Easter Island, however, the schooner sailed first to Tahiti. There the missionaries learned of the December 1862 raid on Easter Island. The situation sounded so grim they changed their minds about going there. Only Brother Eugène Eyraud vowed to continue on. With him traveled Pana, an Easter Islander

Petroglyphs (rock carvings) on Easter Island adorn rocks overlooking the ocean. Islets Motu Nui, Motu Iti, and Motu Kao Kao are in the background (opposite).

who had escaped from his Peruvian captors and fled to Tahiti some time before, bringing news of the raid.

On January 2, 1864, the schooner carrying Brother Eugène and Pana anchored in Easter Island's Hanga Roa Bay. Crewmen in a longboat (small landing craft) rowed the two ashore. Pana carried his few possessions, but Eyraud's things were to be unloaded the next day on another part of the island. They included his books, woodworking tools, a church bell, and five sheep he intended to raise.

Once Brother Eugène and Pana reached land, islanders brandishing sticks and stones surrounded them. While Pana tried to protect Brother Eugène, the islanders stole Pana's belongings.

The next day the schooner came back to Hanga Roa Bay to unload Brother Eugène's luggage. Before he could stop the islanders from rifling through his things, they had made off with his hat, a frock (knee-length) coat, and his five sheep.

Seizing the tools and boards he had brought from Chile, Brother Eugène quickly began to build a small hut. This activity so amused the islanders that they stopped pestering him. When the hut was done, he put a lock on the door and stored what was left of his goods inside before the people could steal those, too.

With the French words Pana had learned in Tahiti, he told Brother Eugène the story of Hotu Matu`a, the islanders' first supreme chief. He took Brother Eugène to the cave at Anakena Beach, where the royal family had first lived, and showed him the stone foundation of the royal dwelling.

After Pana left to rejoin his relatives in a different area of the island, a war chief called Torometi declared himself the missionary's "protector." Torometi's so-called protection consisted mainly of taking any of Brother Eugène's goods he liked, from clothes and tools to a small handbell. One of Brother Eugène's goals as a missionary coming to Easter Island had been to help the people. But he found conditions far worse than he had expected. Smallpox, measles, and other diseases had reduced the number of islanders to about one thousand. Without wise leaders to guide the demoralized population, war chiefs had seized control. Warfare between clans had replaced a more peaceful way of life.

Despite the misery around him, Brother Eugène began his task of converting the islanders to the Roman Catholic religion. He met with some success. As he walked about, curious islanders joined him. When he recited prayers, they seemed willing to recite them, too— maybe, he thought, because the Latin chants sounded like their traditional chants.

Brother Eugène was encouraged. Eventually he taught several of his followers to recite the prayers in Latin. Five or six of his students even learned to read some Latin. He, in turn, was learning to speak the language of the islanders. Soon he knew enough of their language to ask about the strange wooden tablets with carved figures he had seen in people's dwellings. They were rongorongo, he was told, though no one on the island could read them. All of the masters who knew the art of writing and reading the rongorongo had died as slaves in Peru.

After nine months, Brother Eugène had gained a few devoted followers. But most islanders continued to torment him. They forced him to obey them, and like Torometi, they stole from him whenever they had the chance.

More serious trouble erupted after the annual celebration of the birdman god known as Makemake. For two months, groups of islanders had competed in footraces and other activities to honor Makemake. But once the celebration ended, fights broke out. Islanders went on a rampage, plundering and burning the houses of fellow islanders. A gang of marauders attacked Brother Eugène, hitting him with a rock and ripping off his clothing.

He managed to escape and hide in a cave, clad only in an old pair of shoes and a blanket he found. A week later, the schooner captain who had first brought Brother Eugène to the island returned to check on him. Brother Eugène, draped in the blanket, was taken on board to relate his adventures. The horrified captain ignored the missionary's pleas to be put back ashore. Instead he set sail immediately for Chile, with Brother Eugène still aboard.

Seventeen months later, Brother Eugène returned. A French priest, Father Hippolyte Roussel, came with him. Two more missionaries,

The Cult of the Birdman

Sometime in the 1700s, the cult of the birdman began on Easter Island. It was a time of fierce wars between rival groups. People turned from worshiping their ancestors to worshiping the god Makemake, who was half man and half bird. The followers of Makemake believed that he brought birds to the island. So instead of carving stone statues of their ancestors, the people carved pictures of Makemake. There are some five hundred of these stone carvings—called petroglyphs—on the island, mostly in the ceremonial village of Orongo. In July the people held a birdman festival. This was the time when seabirds known as speckled sooty terns came to nest at Motu Nui, an islet one mile off Rapa Nui's southwest coast.

Part of the birdman festival was the egg race. In this grueling contest, each young man who was a hopu manu (a war chief's representative) scrambled one thousand feet down a steep and rocky path to the ocean, paddled on a pora (bundled reed float) through shark-infested waters to the islet, and waited in a cave. When the terns arrived, each young man rushed to find the first egg. The winner shouted to his chief, who was watching from the cliff above, "Shave your head, you have got the egg." He then swam back to Rapa Nui, the egg in a woven basket hung at his neck. If the egg did not break and sharks did not attack the hopu manu, and if he climbed all the way to the top of the sheer cliff without falling, his chief could claim birdman honors.

For the next year, the birdman was treated as a man-god, Makemake's representative on earth. He lived alone, far from his village, and for the entire year did not bathe or cut his hair or fingernails. A servant cooked him special foods, and groups brought gifts and gave him special privileges. After his year was over, he enjoyed a position of respect. The birdman cult, active when the Dutch arrived in 1722, died out after the Catholic missionaries replaced the original rituals, the egg race, and the worship of Makemake with feasting, games, and footraces.

Father Gaspard Zumbohm and Brother Théodule Escolan, followed a few months later. They brought vegetable seeds, saplings, and a few animals. This time the islanders were less hostile to Brother Eugène and helped the missionaries build a church near Hanga Roa Bay.

Soon cattle grazed in a field, fruit trees produced oranges and figs, and corn, pumpkins, and bean plants thrived in the mission garden. The food was a welcome addition to the islanders' meager diet.

Although the people's huts and cave dwellings were scattered over the island, the missionaries encouraged everyone to live near the Hanga Roa mission. They taught the islanders to build wooden houses and make furniture with planks shipped from Chile.

From the start, Brother Eugène and the other missionaries tried to persuade the islanders to give up their beliefs in spirits and Makemake and to accept the Roman Catholic religion. It was not an easy task. Many islanders still spoke of the spiteful tricks the spirits of their ancestors played on them. Often they carried small carved wooden figures with hollow cheeks and protruding ribs that represented the spirits. Brother Eugène once saw an islander dance as he clutched one of these wooden figures and recited a chant in its honor.

On such a small, isolated island there was not much for people to do. Brother Eugène concluded that clan warfare probably helped distract islanders from the predictability of their daily lives. In times of relative peace, the islanders held feasts, and hosts competed to give the most elaborate display of foods.

Father Zumbohm attended one such feast. The host first sent men to catch fish and to fetch potatoes, bananas, sugarcane, and chickens. Then other people dug a pit and made a fire. They wrapped the food in wet grass, placed the wrapped packets in the pit, and covered them with earth and more grass. Guests sat around the fire pit. When the food was cooked, servers placed the best morsels in front of the chief, his special friends, and the guests of honor. No one drank water. To refresh themselves, they sucked on sticks of sugarcane.

When the rat population began to grow, Father Zumbohm made a trip to Chile for some cats. At the same time, he also brought back a shipload of cattle, sheep, horses, pigs, and donkeys. For the first time,

While missionaries tried to convert the islanders from their belief in spirits and Makemake to Christianity, Kava-Kava spirit carvings (left and center) *and Christian statues* (right) *enjoyed equal status among the islanders.*

the islanders saw a man riding a horse. They could scarcely contain their excitement. "Some ran away as fast as they could, others lay on the ground," Father Zumbohm later wrote in a letter. "Those who were sufficiently brave to consider the strange thing a bit closer were not a little amazed when they saw the animal divide into two pieces when the rider dismounted." The islanders were just as astounded by a wheel. When Father Zumbohm loaded his wheelbarrow and began to push it, they "shouted with sheer admiration," he said. "The turning wheel was to them a living thing."

Conversion of the islanders went slowly. The French priests won over the children first, and then the young people and the women. The elders were last to give up their old ways, but in time they, too, embraced the new faith. In August 1868, as Brother Eugène Eyraud lay dying of tuberculosis, the other missionaries consoled him with the fact that, at last, every person on the island had been baptized a Catholic.

Letters and articles written by the Catholic missionaries were excellent sources of information about Easter Island between 1864 and 1872 and about legends from earlier times. In their writings, the missionaries described the daily life of the islanders, the foods people ate, and the games they played. Brother Eugène was the first foreigner to mention the rongorongo tablets, in a letter he sent in December 1864 to church officials. The first published references to the rongorongo tablets came later, in German scientific journals in 1871 and 1872. Brother Eugène was also the first outsider to report hearing the islanders speak of their home as Rapa Nui.

Visit of HMS *Topaze* and the Stolen Friend

The same year that Brother Eugène died, 1868, the British ship HMS *Topaze* anchored in Hanga Roa Bay. After touring the island, the ship's doctor, J. Linton Palmer, spoke with a French priest. When the priest made no mention of giant statues, Palmer assumed the statues were so smashed that the missionaries did not realize what they were.

While on Easter Island, Palmer made several drawings and watercolor paintings, including one of Torometi, Brother Eugène's tormentor. Using Torometi as liaison, Palmer spoke with some islanders. They told him their original home was an island far to the west called Rapa or Rapa Iti (Little Rapa) and that their present home was Rapa Nui (Great Rapa). The name they called themselves, as a group of people, was also Rapa Nui. A few years later, Palmer referred to Rapa Nui in lectures and articles about his visit to the island. It would be many decades, however, before the one-word spelling of Rapanui to refer to both the island and its people became the norm.

During the late 1800s, European explorers were eager to collect works of art from foreign lands. Officers of the *Topaze* hired Torometi

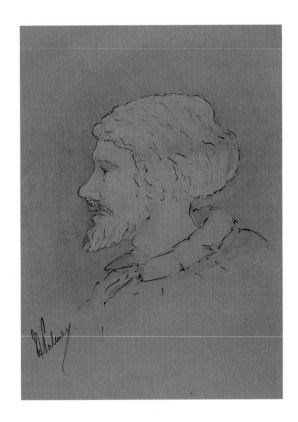

Topaze *ship doctor J. Linton Palmer painted this watercolor of Torometi in 1868. Four years earlier, for a brief time, Torometi had been one of four Easter Island warrior-chiefs.*

to recruit two hundred Rapanui men to help three hundred British sailors remove a stone statue from a house in Orongo, a sacred site at the western point of the island. The huge figure, carved from basalt (volcanic rock), stood eight feet high and weighed four tons. To get it out of the house—which probably had been built around it—the workers had to knock out a wall of the house. Since Orongo was perched on the rim of a volcano, the men had to maneuver the statue down the steep side of the volcano, and then—with the statue's nose scraping the ground—drag it by ropes all the way to the ship. The statue, called *Hoa Hakananai`a* (stolen or hidden friend), was eventually installed in the Museum of Mankind, part of the British Museum in London.

Later in the year, Torometi offered his services to a French adventurer, Jean-Baptiste Dutrou-Bornier, who came to Easter Island to raise sheep and cattle. Torometi arranged for Dutrou-Bornier to "buy" from the Rapanui, for a few pieces of cotton cloth, a parcel of land at Mataveri—the most fertile part of the island.

Dutrou-Bornier had a violent temper. Almost immediately he began to quarrel with the missionaries. He urged Rapanui workers at his sheep ranch to attack the mission at Hanga Roa. The ranch workers began by throwing stones and then burning mission huts. But when the attacks escalated into gunfights, with guns provided by Dutrou-Bornier, the bishop in Tahiti ordered the missionaries to leave. They did. Taking along any Rapanui who wanted to go, the missionaries sailed to Mangareva, an island halfway between Tahiti and Rapa Nui, and started a mission there. Soon after, Dutrou-Bornier's partner in Tahiti, John Brander, sent a ship to Rapa Nui to recruit three hundred islanders to work on Brander's Tahitian plantation. That left only 125 islanders on Rapa Nui. With no way to leave, these people had no choice but to go on working for Dutrou-Bornier.

Selfish and cruel, Dutrou-Bornier treated his workers so unfairly that disgruntled ranch hands eventually killed him. John Brander then hired Alexander Salmon to manage the ranch. Salmon, son of a European trader and a Tahitian princess, had lived and worked on Rapa Nui as a sheep rancher for many years. He sympathized with the Rapanui and spoke their language. He encouraged them to resume carving wooden ancestor spirit figures—an activity the missionaries had forbidden—for trade with visiting ships.

Throughout these troubling times, a few ships—mostly trading vessels bringing goods from Tahiti and picking up meat and wool to take away—still stopped at Rapa Nui. In 1870 the crew of the Chilean ship *O'Higgins* made a survey of the island, which they called Isla de Pascua (Easter Island). While there, crewmen recovered three wooden rongorongo tablets, which were later placed in a museum in Chile's capital city, Santiago.

The islanders who were taken to work in Tahiti kept in touch with family members still in Rapa Nui. A few later returned, including three Rapanui who had contracted leprosy—a skin and nerve disease caused by bacteria—in Tahiti and brought the disease back with them.

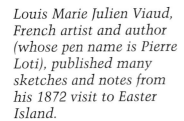

*Louis Marie Julien Viaud,
French artist and author
(whose pen name is Pierre
Loti), published many
sketches and notes from
his 1872 visit to Easter
Island.*

Two years later, in 1872, the French warship *La Flore* made a five-day stop at Rapa Nui while on a training cruise. *La Flore's* admiral was eager to have an ancient statue. He asked one of his cadets, Louis Marie Julien Viaud, to go ashore and find one of a suitable size. Since Viaud knew how to draw, the admiral also asked the young cadet to make sketches of the archaeological ruins.

For the next few days, Viaud explored Rapa Nui—sometimes with a few shipmates. He traveled between ship and shore by whaleboat, returning to the ship for meals and at night. In his notebook, Viaud wrote an account of each day's adventure and made many sketches—some realistic, others depicting ancient times and imagined ceremonies amid rows of upright statues.

Viaud made friends with several young islanders. Occasionally he visited people in their reed huts, where family members shared space with cats, mice, chickens, and rabbits.

He found that the best items for trade with the Rapanui were personal possessions. To acquire a war club, spearheads, and a feathered headdress, Viaud gave up the vest of his uniform, a pair of trousers, and the contents of his pockets—handkerchief, matches, notebook, and pencil. The day before the French ship left Rapa Nui, a work party of one hundred sailors went ashore to collect a giant statue for delivery to a Paris museum. Finding the entire statue far too heavy to move, they sawed off its enormous head—which alone weighed nearly three tons—and took that! In addition, Viaud, with his admiral's permission, obtained a much smaller stone statue from a Rapanui chief. In exchange, Viaud gave the chief the admiral's handsome frock coat.

Viaud later became a popular author, writing under the pen name Pierre Loti. Long after he visited Easter Island, he published notes and sketches from his visit under the title *L'Ile de Pâques, journal d'un aspirant de* la Flore (*Easter Island, Journal of a Young Aspiring Naval Cadet on* La Flore). In it he told how he had gone ashore in his "green youth" but had never forgotten that "half fantastic land . . . of dreams."

⊰ FIVE ⊱

EARLY
REDISCOVERERS

1882–1886

LEXANDER SALMON, WHO HAD COME FROM TAHITI
in 1877 to help run the Rapanui sheep ranch, spoke several
languages and knew the customs of the island. Salmon also
knew the value of ancient island art. So along with working as ranch foreman, he ran an antiques business. He hired islanders
to search caves and hiding places for old ornaments and statues—made
of either stone or wood—which he then sent to Tahiti for sale. Collectors were always eager for artifacts from an exotic place like Rapa
Nui—or Easter Island, as outsiders still called it.

In the late 1800s, a number of collectors who visited the island—
both private individuals and those representing museums—carried
away as many artifacts as they could get their hands on and load onto
a ship. They took mostly small wooden carvings, shells, and human
skulls found at burial sites. Later, they boldly carted away giant

*Over the years, collectors took many items from Easter Island.
This 1885 photograph shows men from the USS* Mohican
removing painted stone slabs from a cave home (opposite).

statues and sections of walls—often doing considerable damage in the process.

Soon, Salmon found himself with yet another job—shepherding visitors around the island. Wilhelm Geiseler, captain of the German steam-powered ship *Hyäne*, arrived in September 1882 on orders from the Ethnology Department of the Berlin Imperial Museum to study the people and artifacts of Easter Island. He hired Salmon to be his guide and interpreter. For a few days, Salmon accompanied Geiseler and his crew. He took them to the ruins of stone statues and platforms along the beach and to Rano Raraku, where the statues had been made.

Wilhelm Geiseler surveyed the quarry and collected stone chisels that had been used to carve the huge figures. He and his fellow Germans estimated that one worker could finish only one or two statues during his lifetime. Later, Geiseler saw the quarry of red tufa (compacted volcanic ash) and realized it was where the islanders found the

This moai is still attached to the rock face at the Rano Raraku (an extinct volcano) quarry.

These adzes (tools for shaping wood) were used by the islanders and are on display at the Bernice P. Bishop Museum in Honolulu, Hawaii.

stone for the huge red "caps" early sea travelers had reported seeing on the statues' heads.

The Germans also investigated the stone houses at the village of Orongo, site of the birdman cult ceremonies. The houses were built of thin, flat slabs of volcanic rock, with layers of stone and earth forming the roof. Low, narrow entrances led inside the small, windowless dwellings. Statues and designs often decorated the small houses, and pictures had frequently been painted on sections of smooth stone that lined the walls and ceilings. Besides copying some of the wall paintings, the Germans tested the stone flooring in one house by hacking it with an ax, presumably to learn if anything was buried underneath. At another house, they tried to remove an interesting statue, but the figure was so heavy that twelve men, using straps and ropes, collapsed under the strain and gave up. The Germans then settled for simply measuring the statue and making sketches of it.

Geiseler paid islanders for permission to dig in burial sites. With pickaxes and shovels, the Germans uncovered fifty skulls, which they added to their growing collection of artifacts from Rapa Nui. Captain Geiseler was disappointed to find no rongorongo boards. He knew of these "talking tablets" from the articles German scientific journals had published in the 1870s. Salmon told the German captain two tablets were still on the island, so Geiseler arranged to buy both and have them sent to the German consul in Chile for shipping on

The village of Orongo consists of large, flat stone buildings constructed on round or oval foundations.

to Germany. Officials at the Imperial Museum in Berlin had given Captain Geiseler a list of objects to collect. But unlike many collectors, Geiseler treated the objects as scientific specimens rather than as curios. He was thorough and precise, describing each item and identifying its importance and how it was used. If he found an interesting article of clothing, he bought not only the garment but also the tools used to work the material and the pigments and dyes used to color it.

Besides studying and collecting island arts and crafts, Geiseler tried to learn as much as possible about the people—their customs for war and peace, their games, and even their methods for naming children. He watched their dances and listened to them sing, collecting samples of play songs, war songs, and love songs. In studying native dances, Geiseler reported on one in which the dancer hops on one foot and jerks the other foot in and out following the rhythm of the song. It was the same kind of dance that the French admiral Dupetit-Thouars had observed on the deck of *La Vénus* nearly half a century before.

Geiseler was interested in island legends and listened as the Rapanui recited legends about the original settlers. One described a large boat arriving from Rapa Nui. Another claimed the first settlers came from the Galápagos Islands. Still others said their ancestors migrated from the west. Geiseler concluded that "to make a definite statement in this regard is rather impossible."

The people told their German visitors about the old days, when they used to catch fish and hold feasts at the high seasons of the year and at the changing of the moon. That was a time, they said, when the land had many people and every foot of ground was used for farming. Geiseler observed that the people could no longer hold such elaborate feasts, because they had barely enough food to feed themselves. Yet they seemed to have little interest in the hard work it took to cultivate the land. There was little evidence of the earlier efforts by outsiders to establish new varieties of plants, trees, and livestock on the island.

Geiseler allowed two hours every day to bargain for goods the islanders wanted to trade. He was helped by Salmon, who knew the standard value of such items. Geiseler tried to obtain an example of

Easter Island artifacts include detailed wood carvings.

every artifact he came across, whether a shell pendant, fishnet, tapa cloth, or a rare kind of reed mat.

At the end of his short visit, Wilhelm Geiseler settled accounts with Salmon, and the *Hyäne* steamed westward toward Samoa. Expedition members' notebooks were bulging with information. In the ship's hold were crates stuffed with everything from stone scrapers, wood carvings, and bone sewing needles to fishhooks, musical instruments, neck pillows, and tools to make butter and cheese.

After returning to Germany, Geiseler published a report on his expedition. His visit to Rapa Nui was notable for several reasons. He brought back more objects than any other collector who had visited the island. He collected not only artwork but also functional items such as tools. And his documentation was outstanding—that is, he took care to describe each object in great detail. But the rongorongo tablets Geiseler had been promised never arrived.

Paymaster Thomson of the USS *Mohican*

Four years later, on December 18, 1886, the American ship USS *Mohican* came to anchor at Easter Island. To the rest of her crew, this may have been just another stop on a Pacific tour, but to William J. Thomson, the ship's paymaster, it was a chance of a lifetime. He had prepared well for it. He was learning the Tahitian language. Earlier, during the *Mohican*'s stopover at Tahiti, he had met with Bishop Jaussen and was permitted to photograph seven rongorongo tablets that Easter Island missionaries had given the bishop in 1868.

Like Geiseler, Thomson hired Alexander Salmon to guide him around the island and act as interpreter. At Salmon's house, Thomson viewed his host's large collection of Easter Island artifacts and arranged to buy some of them.

During his eleven days on the island, Thomson and a work party from the ship circled the island, setting up camp at a new location every day or two. By day Thomson investigated the island—surveying, mapping, and collecting items of interest. In the evenings, he talked with the islanders and Salmon about Rapanui customs, traditions, and legends. With the islanders' help, he compiled a list of fifty-

Crew members from the USS Mohican

seven names of important chiefs, from Hotu Matu`a to the last of the supreme chiefs, Kai Makoi.

At Orongo, the ceremonial village on the rim of a volcano, Thomson inspected the old stone houses. Entering one of these burrowlike structures was not easy. More than once, a lanky sailor got stuck and had to be dragged out by his heels.

Since there were no windows, Thomson used candles for light inside the houses as he made sketches of paintings on the walls. He also had several painted slabs hauled down to the ship.

On another day, the Americans inspected the quarry of red tufa at Puna Pau. From this porous rock the early islanders made the heavy red cylinders that they placed atop many of the statues. Geiseler had called them caps. Thomson called them crowns, or headdresses. Ever since the visit by Captain Cook a century earlier, outsiders had pondered their meaning.

The crater lake at the Rano Raraku quarry

As Paymaster Thomson and his crew made their way around the island, they also explored a number of caves. Many were carved by ocean waves pounding into cliffs. Others were created by a volcanic eruption, when gases in the molten lava expanded to leave open tunnels after the lava hardened.

One of Thomson's tasks was to spend several days excavating parts of the island. He often hired islanders to help his crew with the heavy work. While digging on the north coast at Anakena Beach, where many of the giant statues once stood, the men found grinding stones and broken tools of chipped stone. Under piles of stones where the statues and their red crowns had been toppled and platforms had been destroyed, the Americans discovered human remains. Some were from bodies recently buried; others were ancient bones already crumbling into dust. Thomson compared the entire island to "one vast necropolis [burial-ground]."

Inside the crater at Rano Raraku—the quarry—Thomson and his helpers counted 93 statues. Of these, 40 were standing, finished, and ready to be moved to platforms on another part of the island. The Americans counted 155 more statues on the sloping sides of the volcano. The men also measured the statues. The largest they examined was an unfinished statue seventy feet long and fourteen and a half feet across the body.

Like previous visitors to Easter Island, the Americans found it incredible that the islanders could move such huge figures without any machinery. Thomson estimated that the average statue weighed around twelve tons, with the largest one probably weighing forty tons.

Besides exploring the island and talking with the people, Paymaster Thomson—with the help of Alexander Salmon—also pursued the mystery of the rongorongo tablets. Salmon was able to find and purchase from islanders two rongorongo tablets for Thomson, something he hadn't done for the German visitor Geiseler. One tablet was carved on driftwood, possibly part of a canoe. The other was made from the durable hardwood of an Easter Island toromiro, a small, shrublike tree that was on the verge of extinction.

The messages or stories carved into rongorongo boards centuries ago may hold the key to the Easter Island mystery.

Salmon then introduced Thomson to an elderly Easter Islander, Ure Vaeiko, who as a young boy had studied with a rongorongo master. Thomson and Salmon tried to get the man to read Thomson's newly acquired tablets. The man refused. The Catholic priests forbid reading rongorongo, he said. Then Thomson brought out the photographs he had taken in Tahiti of the bishop's rongorongo tablets. He suggested that the man read one of those. The man had never seen a photograph before, but he recognized one of the tablets, which he said he had known in his young days. Apparently he decided the priests' rule did not apply to the photographs, and he agreed to read it. As he did so, Salmon wrote down the man's words, trying to match them with the symbols. When the old man had been reading for some time, Thomson substituted the second photograph for the first. The man continued telling the same story, not knowing the photographs had been switched. When Thomson and Salmon realized the man was not actually reading the symbols, they accused him of fraud. The man then admitted that he had forgotten the

Tuna fish petroglyph at Tongariki, Easter Island

hieroglyphic symbols and was merely reciting the story as he re-membered it.

Although both Geiseler and Thomson studied the people's lan-guage and customs, Thomson was the first visitor on the island to carryout serious archaeological investigations. While he collected many duplicates of objects Geiseler had found, his investigation was much more complete. Like Geiseler, Thomson did some damage on the island. To learn how the islanders built the stone wall of one of the platforms that held statues, Paymaster Thomson used gunpow-der to blow up a piece of a wall.

On the last day of December 1886, the *Mohican* left the island. Within three years, Paymaster Thomson's long and detailed report was published by the American Museum in Washington, D.C. In his report, Thomson noted that on the walls of some stone houses he saw designs that resembled decorations on pottery he had dug up in the graves of the Incas in Peru. This was the only similarity he found between Rapanui relics and those from the coast of South America.

In 1888 Chile annexed Easter Island—known to the Spanish-speaking Chileans as Isla de Pascua. The islanders continued to call it Rapa Nui. Chile gave a small section of land around Hanga Roa to the islanders to raise crops. A few years later, a British company leased the rest of the land to raise sheep. The company provided jobs to some of the islanders, paying them in pesos. That meant at least a few Rapanui people no longer had to trade for goods. When a Chilean navy ship brought supplies to the company store every two or three years, those islanders who worked on the sheep ranch had money to buy things.

Crew members Charles and Edwin Young on the deck of the vessel Mana. *The name is a Polynesian word for* "good luck."

─ੲ SIX ੪─

THE SEARCH
CONTINUES

1914–1935

I N THE EARLY 1900S, MANY BRITONS WERE FASCI-
nated with the growing science of anthropology—the study
of people and their cultures. Those who could afford it often traveled to foreign lands to study native cultures or to
join archaeological digs and collect ancient artifacts.

In 1910 Katherine and William Scoresby Routledge spent several
months in East Africa on an archaeological mission. So when British
Museum scholars suggested to the Routledges that work remained to
be done on Easter Island—already one of the most famous islands in
the world—the wealthy British couple immediately made plans to or-
ganize an expedition to go there.

By then the mysteries surrounding Easter Island were growing.
Some scholars believed the island was once part of a great sunken
continent. And so far, no one had proved where the first settlers had
come from. Had they sailed from South America, two thousand miles
to the east? Or did the first Easter Islanders fight the prevailing winds
to sail from a Polynesian island to the west?

The Routledges' main goal was to investigate another Easter Island
mystery—how the ancient islanders created and moved the giant
statues. The husband-and-wife team also wanted to study the ahu, or
platforms, on which the statues once stood.

Since William Routledge was an avid sailor, the couple had ship-builders design and build a yacht especially for their expedition. They would call their vessel *Mana*, a Polynesian term that means "good luck." While waiting for the yacht to be built, Katherine Routledge prepared. She spent many hours researching Easter Island at the library of the Royal Geographical Society in London. She learned to speak a few words of Rapanui. And she gathered the supplies they would need—food, cooking pots, tents, camp cots, cameras, surveying equipment, scientific books, and packing materials for skulls and artifacts they might find. Also loaded onto the yacht were reams of paper and quarts of ink Katherine would use for sketches and reports.

Mana sailed from Falmouth, England, on March 13, 1913, with a dozen people on board—a surveyor, a geologist, the Routledges, and a crew consisting of sailing master, navigator, engineer, cook, three seamen, and a cabin boy. Going by way of the Strait of Magellan at the tip of South America, *Mana* reached Easter Island on March 29, 1914—a year after leaving England—and dropped anchor at Hanga Roa Bay on the southern coast of the island.

Members of the *Mana* expedition began their work with a study of the ahu. They set up their first camp at Mataveri on the southwest corner of the island. Each day began with an hour's ride on ponies to one of the 245 ahu scattered along the coast. All of the platforms had

Katherine Routledge

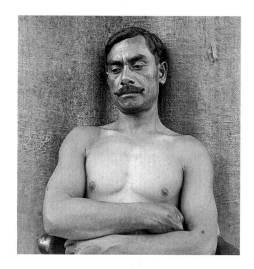

Easter Islander Juan Tepano interpreted for the Routledge expedition.

at least some damage. In front of many ahu, fallen statues lay face-down, "like a row of huge nine-pins." While William Routledge took measurements, Katherine stayed on her pony and took notes on each platform's size and condition. Often she added detailed sketches to her notes. Meanwhile, others made surveys and took photographs.

The Routledges hired Juan Tepano as an interpreter. He was a native islander who had served in the Chilean army and spoke what the Britons called pidgin English—a jargon that was a mixture of Spanish, English, Tahitian, and Rapanui. Katherine Routledge depended on other islanders to serve as guides, too. They told her the names of the monuments and any traditions they could remember. To make sure she was getting all the details, Katherine often asked two different people the same question.

Several ahu were so badly damaged that Katherine could see how they were constructed. Each ahu was like a stone box, with the inside filled with stone rubble and the four sides and the flat top formed by stones fitted together. Some platforms were as wide as fifteen feet, as high as a two-story house, and longer than a football field. From the front of the platform, a ramp made of stones sloped down to a wide stone plaza, or gathering place. Katherine Routledge compared the ahu to a huge stage. She imagined how groups of people might have stood in the plaza long ago, gazing up at the giant statues on the raised platform.

Katherine saw only statues that had been knocked from their ahu.

In the rubble of some of the destroyed ahu, the Routledges discovered skulls and bones.

The ahu were built parallel to the sea. When they were still standing, all of the statues had looked inland, with their backs to the sea. Some platforms had supported as many as fifteen statues.

The islanders told Katherine that the people began to destroy the ahu and moai when the Rapanui chiefs lost their power and war leaders replaced them. Later, the people turned the destroyed monuments into graveyards. Although none of the islanders she talked to remembered seeing a moai actually standing on a platform, many did say that they could still remember when corpses were wrapped in tapa cloth and placed on wooden frameworks a few feet above the broken stones of the destroyed monuments. In time, the wrapped corpse and framework would collapse and settle into the rubble.

For the first two months at the island, *Mana* remained anchored offshore. Then, late in May 1914, *Mana's* crew set sail for Chile to deliver and pick up mail and buy supplies. The round-trip would take nearly three months. Among items to be mailed was an article titled "First Impressions of Easter Island" that Katherine Routledge was sending to the *London Spectator* magazine.

While the yacht was gone, the Routledges and their expedition spent another month or so finishing the work at the ahu. Then they moved to the southeast corner of the island to investigate the quarries. The expedition set up camp at the base of the extinct volcano Rano Raraku. Most of the time, conditions at the Rano Raraku camp were miserable. Cockroaches and flies were everywhere. At mealtime, attacks of mosquitoes and flying beetles sometimes forced campers to wear gloves, stuff their ears with cotton, and cover their heads with mosquito netting as they tried to eat. Even so, Katherine Routledge found the quarry at Rano Raraku to be one of the most spectacular spots on the island.

She and her helpers made a complete survey of the quarry. They counted more than 150 moai, most of them unfinished. On some, only the front and sides had been roughed out. On other statues, the front and sides had been carved and a gutter had been cut out around the figure. Along the gutter, places had been hollowed out to give the carvers a place to stand or squat as they worked. A few statues were finished, except for a narrow strip of uncut stone along the back. The next step would have been to chop away that strip to loosen the statue from the rock so it could be moved from the quarry.

Some moai never made it to the ahu. Instead they ended up on the sloping side of the volcano or on the flat land below. When Katherine's helpers dug around some of the heads poking up through the grass, they discovered complete statues that had been almost covered with rubble and dirt over the years.

The Routledge expedition discovered that, over centuries, dirt and rubble had buried about two-thirds of this moai.

Katherine Routledge had difficulty tracing the exact route the ancient islanders had followed when transporting the statues to the ahu. And no one with the *Mana* expedition managed to solve the problem of how these giant figures were actually moved.

At the end of August 1914, *Mana* returned from Chile with mail and supplies. A week later, the yacht's crew again set sail for Chile with mail from the island to post and another list of supplies to purchase. That fall, before *Mana* had returned, the Routledges learned from a German visitor that Germany was at war with Great Britain and France. Luckily, a Chilean vessel soon called at the island, and William Routledge and the expedition's photographer were able to sail aboard that ship to Chile to look after *Mana*. If Great Britain was at war with Germany, he wanted to buy insurance to protect the ship against war risks.

Since Katherine Routledge and Bailey, the cook, were the only members of the expedition left on the island, they moved back to Mataveri. Bailey provided the meals, while Katherine did more research. With the help of her interpreters, she found out all she could about the birdman cult and the festival that took place each year on the Orongo cliffs. She made twenty visits to Orongo with different Rapanui escorts. She also went three times by boat to Motu Nui, the tiny offshore island to which birdman contestants in the egg race had to swim. Routledge interviewed three islanders who had taken part in the egg race and four who had won the title of birdman for a year.

During her last months on the island, Katherine talked to elderly people at the leper colony. She knew this was almost certainly the last chance they would have to tell their stories. Unsure if she might contract leprosy, Routledge disinfected her clothes and "hoped for the best."

Juan Tepano helped with many of the interviews. Katherine learned what life was like on the island in the 1840s and 1850s, before the first missionaries came and before the Peruvian slave raid. A woman who claimed to be the oldest woman on the island told about going to the birdman festivals and living in one of the stone houses. One man, Te Haha, described feasts he had attended as a young man in the royal court. As *ariki-paka* (member of the aristocratic Miru clan), one of his duties was to pray for rain to make the crops grow. Another man had attended rongorongo school as a boy, and he remembered how the students learned to carve the hieroglyphs using a shark's tooth. He showed Routledge how beginners first practiced on banana stems before they were promoted to carving on the wood they harvested from the few toromiro trees that grew on the west end of the island. An elderly woman sang the same song she had heard sailors from the HMS *Topaze* sing forty-six years earlier, in 1868, as they hauled the stone statue down the mountainside to load onto the ship. The most serious problem with the interviews, Katherine found, was the "constant tendency to glide from what was remembered to what was imagined."

In the fall of 1915, with notes and artifacts, the Routledges

William Routledge took this photograph of two Easter Island women in 1914.

departed for home on their yacht. By early 1916, Katherine Routledge was back in England. She wrote several articles for scientific journals and in 1919 published a book for the general public, *The Mystery of Easter Island: The Story of an Expedition.* Katherine promised to write a "more scientific" account of her work on Easter Island, but she died before she could assemble her notes.

Katherine Scoresby Routledge was the first woman to do scientific studies on Easter Island. Her expedition was the first to make a detailed study of the quarry and the first to provide useful photographs of an investigation on Easter Island. The many excellent black-and-white photographs from the *Mana* expedition provide a permanent record of the monuments on the island in the early 1900s.

Métraux and the French-Belgian Expedition

After the Routledges, others came to probe the secrets of Easter Island. On July 27, 1934, the *Rigault-de-Genouilly*, a French man-of-war, anchored in the bay near Hanga Roa. It remained only long enough to drop off several members of a French-Belgian scientific expedition. A Belgian training ship had agreed to come in six months to give the scientists passage back home.

Heading the group was Swiss-born ethnologist Alfred Métraux, who came to study the islanders' language, legends, customs, and tools. With him came archaeologist Henri Lavachery from Belgium, who wanted to examine the thousands of petroglyphs and other stone works. Israel Drapkin, a doctor, had joined the group in Chile to treat the islanders and collect information about them, as well as to serve as doctor for the expedition.

Despite the rain and the rough seas, French sailors in shore boats deposited the scientists and their ninety packing cases onto the island. Islanders in tattered European shirts and trousers rushed to offer the visitors curios such as feathered headdresses, carved wooden

The islanders used lava rock to make arrowheads.

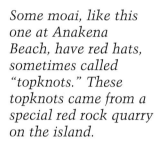

Some moai, like this one at Anakena Beach, have red hats, sometimes called "topknots." These topknots came from a special red rock quarry on the island.

figures, swords and canes, and hats woven by the women of the island. Speaking a mixture of English, French, and Spanish, the islanders asked for soap or clothing in trade.

When Métraux explained that they were archaeologists in search of ancient objects, one of the men said there were not many left. But he assured Métraux that the islanders could make whatever the Frenchman asked for. "When you get home," he said, "nobody will know the difference."

Collecting artifacts was not Métraux's only concern. He had organized the expedition in hope of determining where the first Easter Islanders had come from—Polynesia or the Americas. The French scientist was also eager to find some rongorongo tablets. Would they, he wondered, be evidence of a link between the culture of Easter Island and some advanced civilization in Asia? In the early 1900s, this was a popular theory. One historian at the time saw a resemblance between symbols on the rongorongo and certain Chinese characters.

Métraux hired as his guide and translator sixty-year-old Juan Tepano, who had worked for Katherine Routledge twenty years before. Tepano provided the visitors with useful information about the islanders and their history. Tepano's aging mother was one of the few islanders at the time of Métraux's visit who still understood the ancient words and had experienced the traditional culture before the Peruvian slave raid of 1862.

While Dr. Drapkin spent his time in and around Hanga Roa, Métraux and Lavachery measured and described statues and ruins. Lavachery estimated the islanders took one month to roughly carve a large moai, ready to be finished. Katherine Routledge, twenty years earlier, figured the process took fifteen days.

To help understand the past, Métraux learned the islanders' Rapanui language, which he classified as Polynesian. He studied the legends of Hotu Matu`a and the ariki, or sacred chiefs, who followed. As the islanders told Métraux stories about their ancestors, he concluded the ancient islanders must have enjoyed a well-balanced diet. In every story he heard, there seemed to be a list of the foods people ate—yams, taros, potatoes, chickens, eels, spiny lobsters, and fish.

From his interviews, Métraux learned a great deal about the people's daily activities and their language and legends. In studying the legends about wars, feuds, and acts of revenge, Métraux concluded that the people gave up their statue building and peaceful ways and turned to warfare in the late 1700s. That was why he found no weapons in the quarries—but elsewhere he collected many weapons, such as spears with obsidian (glassy lava rock) points, clubs, and stones that could be hurled at the enemy.

Métraux compiled a list of supreme chiefs who succeeded Hotu Matu`a. By allowing twenty-five years for each reign, he decided that the first settlers must have arrived in the 1100s—and that the first statues were erected shortly after Hotu Matu`a's landing. Métraux disagreed with theories that the red topknots represented bleached hair, hats, or wigs. He felt they were simply an attempt to give a bit of decoration to the images and add an amusing, more natural, touch.

Métraux saw only two persons with tattoos during his visit, both very old women, which he took as proof that the islanders had given up tattooing after the French missionaries arrived in 1864. One of the women, who was born around 1830, had her legs tattooed as if she were wearing tights. The other, Ana Eva Hei (Queen Eva), who was born around 1840 and had been the wife of one of the last supreme chiefs of Easter Island, had her forehead, ear, lower jaw, and hands tattooed.

One question Métraux was not able to answer was how the early islanders could build—without trees—the skids or rollers they would have needed to transport the statues. He decided that at some time

This head at Tahai is said to be the oldest on Easter Island.

all the trees must have been destroyed. The island appeared to be fertile, and visitors during the 1700s and 1800s had written about the rich volcanic soil, the green meadows, the gardens, and the banana plantations. The only things the island seemed to lack—according to these early visitors—were trees.

When the six months were up, Alfred Métraux realized he had not allowed enough time to do all the archaeological studies he would have liked. Even so, he felt his study of Easter Island had been thorough. "I doubt that a longer visit would have added much to my material," he said.

As planned, the Belgian training ship *Mercator* arrived to pick up the scientists on January 2, 1935. In the dozens of cases loaded onto the ship were artifacts the expedition had collected, along with the notes Métraux would sort through when he returned home. In 1940 Métraux published *Ethnology of Easter Island*. In the report, Métraux summarized all that was known about Easter Island up to that time.

Father Sebastian Englert, a German monk, on Easter Island in the 1930s

—— ⊰ SEVEN ⊱ ——

METHODS OLD
AND NEW

1935–1975

B Y THE EARLY 1930S, THERE WERE 456 RAPANUI ON the island. Most lived in or near Hanga Roa. Twenty-two who suffered from leprosy were confined to a hut about two miles north of the village. A barbed-wire fence separated the part of the island where the Rapanui lived from the sheep ranch, and only Rapanui who worked there were allowed on the ranch. A few had low-paying jobs as guards. Some others, hired each spring to shear sheep, earned even less. They were paid according to the number of animals they sheared.

Shearing time was an important event, since it broke the monotony of daily life. Young people competed to see who could shear the most sheep. Although this replaced the old native feasts, which had competitions of a different sort, it was not enough to give the people a sense of community. Besides losing touch with past rituals and customs, many Rapanui had abandoned the religion of the French missionaries. Through the years, spiritual leaders among the Rapanui had tried to take over the role of priest and revive the teachings of the Catholic Church. But the islanders were too demoralized to listen. When Métraux arrived in 1934, he was appalled at the poverty. He called Easter Island "undoubtedly the most unhappy of all the Pacific colonies . . . isolated and neglected."

Chile forbade the Rapanui people to leave the island but took little interest in their welfare. The islanders had no hospital or regular school for the children. Even though Chilean teachers arrived from time to time, none stayed for long. For many Rapanui, life was little more than a struggle to exist until the next ship arrived. Meanwhile, they wove baskets or carved small wooden statues and other curios to barter for soap, clothing, salt, and other goods. Unfortunately it could be months—or even years—between ships' visits.

Work of Father Sebastian

In 1912 Sebastian Englert of Germany was ordained as a Capuchin monk—a Franciscan monk who is dedicated to missionary work among the poor. In 1922, at his own request, Father Sebastian was sent to Chile as a missionary to the Araucaniane Indians. There he studied languages of both the Araucanianes and the Rapanui and published several works. In 1933 he visited Easter Island. What Father Sebastian saw so distressed him that two years later, in 1935, he volunteered to be a missionary on Rapa Nui. Once installed on the island, in addition to being the parish priest, he continued to learn as much as he could about the language. He remained the people's priest on Rapa Nui the rest of his life.

Unlike slavers and others who mistreated the islanders, Father Sebastian cared deeply about the Rapanui people. He proved to be a friend they could trust. He encouraged them to return to the Catholic religion. Before long, Sunday morning church service and the dinner that followed became the event of the week for the islanders.

When Father Sebastian first arrived on the island, he lived at the leper colony for several weeks. He talked with many old men and women there about the island's history. The Rapanui followed a custom of memorizing the names of their illustrious ancestors. Some old-timers at the leper settlement could recite the names of important chiefs back to the direct descendants of Hotu Matu`a. Father Sebastian found the oldest leper at the colony, Arturo Teao, to be the most helpful in recalling names and events from the past.

After Father Sebastian moved to Hanga Roa, he continued to

The interior of the Easter Island leprosy settlement, 1930s

research the history of the people and their language, as well as tend to his congregation. His only contact with the outside world came when an occasional ship visited the island, and once a year when a Chilean warship arrived. In 1934 the Chilean navy had taken over management of the sheep ranch. From then on, warships made yearly visits to bring food and other necessities to the islanders, drop off and pick up mail, and collect bales of wool from the sheep ranch.

Living in such a remote location, Father Sebastian was free to concentrate his attention on what he saw and heard on the island. He quickly became fluent in Rapanui, and he compiled a Rapanui dictionary and grammar book. Over time he collected enough songs, legends, and other information to publish several more books and articles about the island's history and traditions. Father Sebastian admitted that all he knew came from what the islanders told him, from reading the works of others, and from what he observed. He did not pretend that he had the final word on a subject, and he knew that future research might prove him wrong. "Development of knowledge," he said, "consists of the constant correction of errors . . . and when the subject is enigmatic Easter Island, no man's knowledge is complete or secure."

Father Sebastian found that the islanders often mixed made-up stories with genuine oral history, for it was hard to resist adding extra details to make a good story even better. Even so, he believed that every legend contained a grain of truth.

He heard many legends about the supreme chief Hotu Matu`a, who left his home in Hiva and came with his family by giant canoe to the island they called Te Pito te Henua (navel of the earth). The priest was convinced that these first settlers came from Polynesia—and when one legend told of them sailing toward the sun, it meant the rising sun. From "ancestor lists" he compiled, Father Sebastian calculated that Hotu Matu`a arrived at Easter Island in the 1500s. (Later tests in the 1970s with radiocarbon dating would suggest that people lived on the island as long ago as the 800s, and possibly even earlier.)

Father Sebastian came to the conclusion that fighting broke out among the clans between 1771 and 1773. This supports Métraux's theory and fits in with the fact that Roggeveen and González saw no fighting, but Captain Cook, who arrived in 1774, found signs that the people had suffered from some sort of serious conflict.

Through his writings and lectures, Father Sebastian introduced Rapanui legends and customs to outsiders. He explained the Rapanui people's belief in spirits and in the importance of *tapu* (taboo)—things they should not do. Early islanders believed that their chiefs held spiritual power over the vegetable and animal kingdoms, and it was this mana that made crops grow and assured an abundance of fish in the sea.

Like other outsiders, Father Sebastian was amazed at the islanders' love of hats, and their use of hats to express feelings. For example, the Rapanui often wore a certain kind of hat with two long feathers that hung down in front. But if a man became angry with someone, he wore his hat so the feathers hung behind.

Late in 1955, a gleaming white trawler steamed into the bay off Hanga Roa and dropped anchor. On board, besides the crew of thirteen, were Norwegian explorer and investigator Thor Heyerdahl, his wife, Yvonne, their two-year-old daughter and teenage son, five archaeologists (three from the United States, one from Norway, and another from Chile), a doctor, and a photographer. Among the supplies they had brought from Norway were cloth for barter, an ample supply of meals for everyone, and spades and shovels. This archaeological expedition had not come "to study the natives," said Heyerdahl. They had come "to dig."

Waiting to welcome the group when they came ashore stood a tall man with a flowing beard and wearing a long white monk's robe: Father Sebastian. Heyerdahl explained their plans, and the priest described his own research. Along with his research into the language

Thor Heyerdahl, a Norwegian explorer, tried to solve the mystery of how the huge statues may have been moved to and placed upon the platforms.

and legends, Father Sebastian had made a thorough study of the ahu and had marked every statue with a number. He worked closely with the Heyerdahl expedition during its stay. He offered advice, helped find workers, and made suggestions.

The Norwegian expedition chose to set up camp on the north shore of Easter Island, near Anakena Beach. The nearest sources of water were marshes in the craters of three old volcanoes, four miles away. The only wood came from a eucalyptus grove at the sheep ranch, which had been planted by Europeans a few years earlier. Fortunately, once the men unloaded the expedition's jeep from the trawler, collecting a daily supply of firewood and water was no problem.

Their first excavation was at Anakena—where, according to legend, Hotu Matu`a had first landed. A foot below the surface, the men found fishhooks made of human bone and spearheads. Digging deeper, they found more fishhooks, human teeth, and blue beads. Heyerdahl thought they might be the beads Roggeveen had given to the islander who came aboard the Dutch ship in 1722.

These researchers were the first on the island to establish dates of certain events or artifacts by carbon-14 dating. This is a method for determining the date at which organic material (such as a plant or animal) was formed. It is done by measuring the ratio between two forms of carbon—one that decays over time and one that does not.

From evidence found at various excavations, Heyerdahl's archaeologists established three important periods for the early islanders:
1. the Early Period (sometime before A.D. 800 to around 1100), when people constructed the ahu;
2. the Middle Period (between approximately 1100 and 1680), when people built the giant statues; and
3. the Late Period (between 1680 and around 1868), when people destroyed the statues and ahu, fought one another in wars, and began using the wrecked ahu as burial sites.

Members of the Norwegian expedition were the first to discover the history of the island's environment through pollen testing. They made test borings in swamps in three volcano craters and claimed to have found the pollen of the same kind of totora reed that also grows in Peru.

While working at the Rano Raraku quarry, expedition members discussed how long it might have taken the early islanders to carve a giant statue. Father Sebastian estimated somewhere between a few months and a year. The archaeologists decided to put the question to a practical test. Heyerdahl hired six islanders. They were to use the same tools their ancestors had once used—stone picks made from basalt, a very hard volcanic stone. And they were to outline a statue sixteen feet long on the same type of volcanic rock the ancients had used—tuff (sometimes called tufa). The rock is extremely hard on the surface, but beneath the hard outer layer is a layer of compressed ash that is not much harder than chalk. Carving it is much like working with wood. After a week or so, when the carved areas are exposed to the weather, they begin to harden. For months and even years after, they continue to get even harder.

Amid clouds of dust, the workers chipped at the stone. They had to stop often to sharpen their blunted picks. To soften the tuff, they splashed water on it. When the stone figure began to take shape after three days, the men were tired and ready to stop. Considering how long it had taken them to shape the figure, various observers calculated how long it might take six men working all day in shifts to finish a medium-sized statue. Pedro Atan, mayor of the island, settled on twelve months, and William Mulloy, one of the American archaeologists with the expedition, agreed.

Next came the question of how the ancients transported their statues. Some islanders said it was the early priests' mana. Supposedly the mana enabled the statues to walk a short distance each day until they finally reached their platform on the seacoast. Heyerdahl's group had a different theory. To test it, they recruited a huge group of volunteers by holding a great feast for the islanders, with music, dancing, roasted oxen, sweet potatoes, corn on the cob, and baked pumpkins. Then, urged on by the mayor, some two hundred willing volunteers teamed together to pull a recently excavated statue. The statue weighed around ten or twelve tons—about the same as five or six medium-sized cars. On the first try, the rope around the statue's neck broke. The ropes were doubled and reattached. This time the

The Fierce Battle of Poike Ditch

A Rapanui legend made popular by Father Sebastian told of two groups of islanders—the hanau eepe, *or "long ears," and the* hanau momoko, *or "short ears." Father Sebastian preferred to translate* hanau eepe *as "corpulent or fat" and* hanau momoko *as "thin or slender."*

After the hanau momoko first settled the island, the hanau eepe arrived. Father Sebastian believed that the newcomers, the hanau eepe, built the first great ahu, but the original colonists, the hanau momoko, were the first to carve the great stone images of their dead ancestors. Later, the hanau eepe began carving the huge stone statues also.

After the supreme chief Hotu Matu`a died, the two groups became bitter enemies. Around 1680 they engaged in a fierce battle at Poike Ditch. The hanau eepe intended to throw the hanau momoko into a ditch filled with burning brush and dry grass, but the plan backfired, literally, when the hanau momoko learned of the plot. They managed to trap the hanau eepe and throw them into the flames instead. Supposedly, only one hanau eepe survived.

Paymaster Thomson first heard the story from his guide, Alexander Salmon, in 1886. Later, Katherine Routledge was told two versions, and Métraux also heard—but did not believe—the story. In the 1940s, Father Sebastian met a man who claimed that he descended from that lone survivor of the Poike Ditch massacre. Father Sebastian counted the generations back from this man. Allowing fifteen years for each generation, he determined the actual date of the battle to be 1680. This was very close to the date— 1676 plus or minus ten years—that Thor Heyerdahl came up with by doing radiocarbon dating of charcoal samples from the trench.

Some time after this battle, Jacob Roggeveen, the first of Easter Island's European visitors, arrived there. According to stories collected by Father Sebastian, the lone survivor of the Poike Ditch massacre was the same man who first went aboard Roggeveen's ship to greet the Dutch explorers.

With many workers, ropes, poles, and rocks, Heyerdahl could successfully move and raise a moai. Perhaps this was how the early islanders had erected their statues.

jubilant islanders succeeded. The statue moved! The Rapanui men and women did not pull it very far, but they proved it could be done.

On another occasion, the mayor demonstrated to Heyerdahl how his ancestors used only rocks, ropes, and wooden poles to lift the huge moai onto the ahu. The mayor assembled a dozen islanders at an ahu in Anakena, where a fallen statue lay. This statue weighed perhaps twenty-five tons. Using the poles as levers, eleven of the mayor's helpers raised the giant by stages, a fraction of an inch at a time. As the space under the statue widened, the twelfth man—the mayor's brother—pushed stones between the statue and the ground. As the figure rose higher, the pile of supporting stones grew larger. Finally, after eighteen days, the group had the moai upright on the ahu.

Heyerdahl realized that placing a red topknot onto a giant statue must have been just as difficult, since some topknots weighed close to eleven tons. He assumed the workers must have built a stone ramp that sloped up to the top of the statue and then rolled the heavy cylinder up the ramp.

Both Heyerdahl and Father Sebastian believed the hundreds of workers who carved and transported the giant statues received as pay plenty of nourishing food—and that the rest of the islanders raised crops and caught fish to support the work. The carvers and movers also believed the gods would treat them kindly and grant them super-natural benefits for their labors.

An important goal of Heyerdahl's was to find proof that the island's early settlers came from South America rather than Polynesia. In his book *Kon Tiki*, published three years earlier, Heyerdahl had compared early Polynesians with South Americans and found they had many similar physical characteristics, legends, religious views, boatbuilding techniques, and stone sculptures. Although *Kon Tiki* was a best-seller, many scientists criticized Heyerdahl for ignoring evidence that contradicted his theory. Nevertheless, Heyerdahl persisted. On Easter Island, he found signs he was sure pointed to an Easter Island–South American connection. At the ancient ahu at Vinapu, he discovered squared volcanic stones fitted together as precisely as those he had seen on stonework in the Bolivian Highlands of South America.

While excavating on another part of the island, expedition archaeologists Arne Skjølsvold of Norway and Gonzalo Figueroa of Chile found a statue of a kneeling man unlike any other giant figures on Easter Island. The man had a round head, goatee, and normal-sized ears, while most other huge statues on the island were torsos of beardless men with deep-set eyes, somber expressions, and elongated heads and ears. Again Heyerdahl wondered: Was the kneeling man Polynesian or South American?

After five months, the Norwegian expedition left Rapa Nui to spend time studying other Polynesian islands. On his return to Norway, Heyerdahl told of his Easter Island adventures in *Aku-Aku*, another book that became a best-seller. He also wrote several more scholarly books on his theories about the original Easter Islanders and his scientific findings.

In the 1950s, German linguist Thomas M. Barthel visited Rapa Nui to study the legends and ancient language of the islanders. For years, Barthel had tried to solve the riddle of the rongorongo tablets. Although Barthel figured the 120 basic designs could be combined to create up to 2,000 new symbols, he was unable to decipher the mysterious writing.

Father Sebastian had also tried to solve the rongorongo mystery. He had concluded that the answer had gone to the grave with the last

As Heyerdahl's crew members kept digging deeper and deeper, they discovered a statue different from all others on the island—a kneeling moai.

of the religious leaders. One problem for Barthel and other scholars was that there were so few tablets to study. In museums throughout the world there existed fewer than thirty rongorongo boards.

Restorations Begin

In 1960 a powerful tsunami (a tidal wave caused by a powerful earthquake—in this case, in Chile) struck the south coast of Easter Island. It destroyed Ahu Tongariki and scooped up several of the fallen sixty-ton statues, tossing them as far as one hundred yards inland. Soon after, the University of Chile in Santiago sent a group to another part of the island to restore monuments that were damaged long ago by islanders during the statue-toppling time.

By 1960 researchers could visit Rapa Nui much more easily than their predecessors. Chile had begun air travel between Rapa Nui and the mainland in 1951, when a Catalina (or "flying boat") flew 2,047 miles in seventeen hours to land on a field between Hanga Roa and Mataveri. A few years later, the Chileans built an airstrip on the island so regular planes could land.

Heading the restoration group were three archaeologists—Americans William S. Ayres and William Mulloy and Gonzalo Figueroa of Chile. Mulloy and Figueroa had visited the island earlier as part of

This moai, already toppled at some earlier time, is one of many statues on the ground at Tongariki. The statues were tossed inland by the powerful 1960 tsunami.

the Norwegian expedition. To erect the toppled statues at Ahu Akivi—located near the craters of the three old volcanoes and one of the few inland ahu—the group used the same means the expedition had tried while re-erecting a single statue five years before—levers and stones.

That same year, William Mulloy and others formed the Easter Island Statue Project to study all of the statues by modern archaeological methods. American archaeologist Patrick C. McCoy assumed command of the fieldwork. To give each team of fieldworkers an area of manageable size to study, McCoy divided the island into thirty-five sections, with each team responsible for a square section measuring less than two miles on a side. Within that section, the team members described and marked the locations of houses, roads, platforms, fallen or buried statues, and other features. They took measurements and photographs, made sketches, and wrote detailed notes.

After a year, the fieldworkers put aside the survey to help Mulloy's group excavate and restore monuments on other parts of the island, including those at a ceremonial site at Tahai on the western shore, near Hanga Roa. Sometimes cranes were used to help maneuver the massive stones in place, but the procedure was costly—up to five thousand dollars to raise a statue and four times as much to rebuild a platform. By this time, the government of Chile had declared Easter

Island a national monument, so various government and private groups contributed money to help pay for restorations.

Father Sebastian was eager to do his part to protect Easter Island's art and architecture and to support the restorations. Although he had become ill and quite frail, he embarked on a speaking and fund-raising tour in the United States late in 1968. On January 8, 1969, while in New Orleans, the priest died of cancer at age eighty.

Work on the island continued. Archaeologist William S. Ayres determined through radiocarbon dating in 1971 that the huge statues on the island were carved and put in place between the years 1100 and 1555. In the meantime, American and Chilean archaeologists continued to excavate and restore platforms. Fieldworkers from the University of Chile took over the survey project in 1975.

The first flight to Easter Island took place in January 1951. Chilean Air Force Amphibian PBY-5A has Manu-Tara (Good Luck Bird) painted on its side.

Petroglyphs at Orongo

—⋙ EIGHT ⋘—

FILLING IN THE GAPS

T HE FIRST VISITORS TO EASTER ISLAND JOTTED down their impressions in letters, journals, and ships' logs. Few of these outsiders stayed long enough to do much exploring. Some did not even go ashore—they simply observed the island from the ship's deck. Even so, their eyewitness accounts and occasional sketches are important, for these first impressions provide the only descriptions of the island in the 1700s. These early reports give an idea of how the people looked, what they did, the foods they ate, what animals lived on the island, and what plants grew there. And always there was mention of the mysterious giant statues on their wide platforms.

Later on, reports were more detailed. They described not only the statues and platforms, but also the quarries, the stone houses at Orongo, and the petroglyphs. Then collectors arrived. They carted away tools, ornaments, woodcarvings, the occasional rongorongo tablet, and even sections of stone walls and large statues. Meanwhile, scholars came to study the language of the ancient islanders and gather information on legends and traditions. By the early 1900s, photographs of islanders and island art appeared.

Modern-day researchers are filling in the gaps left in earlier reports. By 1981, after the University of Chile took over the survey project

Jo Anne Van Tilburg divides this moai into a grid that will help create an exact computer image of the statue.

begun by William Mulloy, American and Chilean fieldworkers had surveyed more than half of the island and had located 675 statues, including 397 that were still in the quarry where they were carved.

Various people have demonstrated different ways the early islanders might have moved the moai. In 1982 Pavel Pavel, a Czech engineer, built a concrete replica of a moai and attached ropes to the head and base of the upright figure. Then two teams of helpers pulled on the ropes and tilted and rocked the statue back and forth and thus managed to move it a few yards on level ground. When Norwegians Thor Heyerdahl and Arne Skjølsvold began their 1986–1987 Norwegian expedition to Easter Island, they invited Pavel to try out his experiments on a real stone statue. Pavel did, and he was able to move it a short distance.

In the 1980s, American geologist Charles Love also used a concrete replica of a statue to test his theory of how the moai were moved. Love placed his statue upright on a platform that consisted of two logs carved into sled-runners. With helpers, he placed statue and sled platform onto log rollers. A crew of twenty-five men easily pulled the statue along a level path, traveling 148 feet in two minutes.

In the early 1990s, archaeologist Jo Anne Van Tilburg applied computer modeling to test her theory. Since 1982 Van Tilburg had been directing a project on Rapa Nui to study the statues, which had yielded precise measurements of hundreds of statues. These she entered into a computerized database.

From information in the database, Van Tilburg and computer experts at the robotics lab of the University of California at Los Angeles created a computer model of an average-sized statue. They concluded that such a statue could have been moved from quarry to ahu with a crew of seventy men. Each man's nutritional requirements "would have been 2,880 calories per day, of which he would have expended roughly fifty percent in energy," Van Tilburg said. She believed the statues were moved on their backs—probably resting on two crossbeams placed on two transport beams, which in turn were placed over several wooden rollers.

In 1998 Van Tilburg tested her theory on Rapa Nui, using a ten-ton concrete replica of a moai. After some changes in the transport rig and a last-minute switch from rolling the rig on wood rollers to sliding it on wood rails, between fifty and sixty Rapanui were able to successfully pull the replica about one hundred yards. A group of twenty Rapanui later raised it upright onto a platform. Van Tilburg concluded that although her method of transporting the statue needed work, her projections of time, resources, and people required to move the average statue were largely verified.

Scholars and scientists continue to use radiocarbon dating to piece together information about life on Easter Island in earlier times. They believe the first ceremonial platforms—the ahu—were built before A.D. 1000. Gradually, larger and more elaborate platforms replaced these simple structures. The people carved most of the statues and placed them on the ahu between about 1000 and 1500—more than two hundred years before the first Europeans saw them. According to prehistorian Paul Bahn and ecologist and geographer John Flenley, the "building of platforms seems to have become an obsession" by 1200, and this "golden age"—the peak construction time for both platforms and statues—lasted well into the 1500s.

Scientists estimate that around 1550 the population of the island was between seven thousand and nine thousand people—nearly all of

Patricia Vargas Casanova and other archaeologists from the University of Chile dig at the site of an ancient house on Easter Island.

them involved in the "statue cult." Over time the statue-making became more ambitious as clans competed to build ever-larger statues, often adding massive red topknots. Bahn and Flenley suggest that the *pukao*, the large red cylinders atop the heads of some statues, were a late addition—perhaps a way for rival villages or kin groups to "outdo each other in the splendour of their monuments."

Flenley and others believe that to support this frenzy of statue-building, the people began to cut down more and more trees—for rollers to transport the giant figures and poles to raise them onto the ahu, and for cooking fuel. At first, fewer trees gave the people more room to grow food to keep the hardworking stone carvers and movers well nourished.

In time, though, the people cut down so many trees that they altered the ecology of the island. Changes in climate reduced the amount of food they could grow. Without wood to build canoes, the people could no longer go out into the ocean for additional food. Food shortages developed, the population decreased, and the pace of statue-building slowed. Eventually fights broke out between clans. Clan members of high rank—such as the Miru, who lived around Anakena and who claimed to be direct descendants of Hotu Matu`a—banded together. They began to oppose those of lower rank, who lived on the other side of the island and were mostly workers. By the mid-1600s, the clan chiefs lost control over their members, and warriors became the leaders. During this period, the islanders began to destroy the statues of their enemies and to abandon their statue cult to embrace a new religion—that of Makemake.

Easter Island researchers have a good idea of when these activities occurred. In 1770, when ships from Spain arrived, islanders joined the sailors and priests in a procession across the island. They were chanting, "Makemake," although the Spanish did not know what this meant. Around the same time, the islanders must have also just begun toppling the statues of their enemies, because the Spanish visitors did not mention seeing fallen statues. Four years later, members of Captain Cook's expedition reported many overturned statues.

Experts are also learning about the diets and social practices of islanders who lived in the late 1600s and early 1700s. They study Xrays of their bones and skulls. The Routledges had sent fifty-eight skulls back to England to be studied by Sir Arthur Keith, British anatomist (anatomy expert), who found tooth decay in every adult skull he examined. More recent osteologists (bone specialists), including Dr. David Owsley of the Smithsonian Institution, confirm Keith's findings. They suspect the many cavities of these early islanders were caused by a sugar-heavy diet of sugarcane, sweet potatoes, and taro. Otherwise, the people were fairly healthy. Although many of the skulls the doctors examined have depression fractures, the fractures were not serious and apparently healed quickly. This meant that although the people were probably in many fights, few of them died as a result. Some of the legends about great battles may have been exaggerated, since experts saw little evidence of "fight to the finish" events. Perhaps as the early islanders repeated stories over and over, occasional killings became magnified into battles of major proportions.

Physical anthropologists, who study physical traits of humans and how they developed, are also learning about the ancient islanders. In testing skeletons from various parts of the island, they found evidence that islanders from different groups had different physical traits. For example, all of the people from Anakena had kneecaps with a corner missing. Skeletons from other parts of the island did not have this trait. This finding appears to confirm that people living around Anakena, the legendary home of Hotu Matu`a, were either his descendants or members of the high-status Miru clan. Since the Miru did not tolerate outsiders and married only within their group, the result probably was inbreeding that produced a gene pool with little variety. That could be why everyone at Anakena ended up with the same kind of kneecap.

In another recent excavation at Anakena, Chilean archaeologist Claudio Cristino discovered dog bones. Cristino's findings indicate that the first settlers probably brought dogs as well as chickens and edible Polynesian rats. These small, mouse-sized rats were considered a delicacy by the elders. The rats lasted only until the larger European ship rats replaced them, but the chickens survived through modern times. The dogs did not.

A view of the modern-day village of Hanga Roa, from the waterfront

A store on Easter Island serves as a gathering place for the residents there.

Present-day researchers study many other aspects of Rapanui life, past and present. Since 1981 American archaeologist and art historian Georgia Lee has worked on a project to document the island's many petroglyphs, and in 1990 she published a guide to the island and its archaeological mysteries. Australian anthropologist Grant McCall spent time living and working with the Rapanui. In 1994 he wrote a book, *Rapanui: Traditions and Survival on Easter Island*, about the modern society and how the people have dealt with change. McCall has also studied the pattern of drought periods on the island.

Some modern researchers are finding out about the kinds of plants that grew on the island long ago. Paleontologists, who study ancient plants and animals, begin their research by collecting samples of sediment deep in the ground. They bore deep into the boggy marshes in the island's crater lakes and then examine the columns of sediment they bring up. At the top of the column are the most recent layers of dirt. Farther down are older deposits of sediment. With radiocarbon testing, the scientists figure out the age of each layer. Next, with a powerful microscope, they study the pollen grains of a particular layer. They sort, count, and identify types of pollen. This tells them which plants grew on the island in ancient times.

When John Flenley and Sarah King did pollen analysis on Easter Island, they discovered that the island had once had a subtropical forest containing ferns, herbs, grasses, woody bushes, and several different types of trees. The two researchers found that the palm tree, extinct from the island, once grew in great profusion and was closely related to the Chilean wine palm—which grows up to eighty-two feet tall and six feet in diameter. The trunks of palm trees would have made perfect roller logs to move the statues and could have been what the early islanders used. The tall, unbranched trunks of palms could also have been used to build large canoes.

DNA tests in 1994 may have helped scientists decide the long-debated question of where the original settlers came from. Four DNA experts from England, Chile, and Spain tested bones that Heyerdahl and his team of archaeologists took from two different sites on Easter Island during the 1955–1956 expedition. The experts extracted DNA from the bone samples and compared the DNA with that of present-day Polynesians. They believe the results confirm a connection between the two, and therefore, that the original settlers were Polynesian. Despite the fact that the bones in the study had been examined by several groups of physical anthropologists without special precautions to avoid contamination, the DNA testers said, "unambiguous [clear] genetic information could be recovered from them."

Modern-day researchers believe they have resolved the issue of the great Poike Ditch battle. According to legend, the islanders known as "short ears" massacred all but one of an enemy group known as "long ears." Using radiocarbon dating, however, archaeologists determined great fires occurred in the ditch five hundred years before the supposed Poike Ditch battle around 1680. They believe the area was merely a place where cooks used several earth ovens to prepare food for the stone carvers, or possibly it was where early islanders burned stalks and leaves. Another reason some archaeologists are skeptical about legends of a Poike Ditch battle is that they have found no human remains or spear points in Poike Ditch.

References to cannibalism (eating human flesh) abound in island legends. According to Métraux, in every traditional legend, he heard about a battle at the end of which "the vanquished took refuge in caverns where the victors sought them out. The men, women, and children who were captured were eaten." The islanders showed Katherine Routledge a cave in Malaveri, near Orongo, which they

Archaeologists from the University of Chile excavate across Poike Ditch.

called Ana Kai Tangata (Eat-man Cave). They told Routledge that cannibal feasts were held there during the birdman rites. During Heyerdahl's excavations in caves, his archaeologists found bones from fish, fowls, rats, turtles, and humans. They also found several dozen needles made from human bones.

Other archaeologists, though, say they have seen little evidence that cannibalism occurred over a wide area—if it occurred at all. John Flenley points out the translation of the Rapanui words Ana Kai Tangata could equally be "place where men eat." French archaeologists Catherine and Michel Orliac suggest cannibal feasts were reserved for military chiefs and their warriors. Jo Anne Van Tilburg agrees but feels that widespread cannibalism remains "a matter of speculation" and has yet to be "demonstrated archaeologically."

As scientists and scholars continue working on the island, some start new projects. Others try to fine-tune work begun earlier. In the 1970s, while directing the restoration of fallen statues at an ahu near Anakena, Rapanui archaeologist Sergio Rapu Haoa uncovered part of an ahu wall and a walkway leading to it. Later excavations of the site by Rapu, Arne Skjølsvold, and others on the 1986–1987 Norwegian expedition uncovered many dolphin bones, among other things. In early times, eating dolphin was tapu for people other than chiefs, so these bones could mean that the settlement was associated with leading chiefs and priests, rather than ordinary people. The bones also suggest the use of big seaworthy vessels, since dolphins generally live far out at sea and cannot be hunted from shore.

Chisels, scrapers, drills, and files found in the same place indicate wooden idols were made there. The burned obsidian disc they found—perhaps an eye pupil of a wooden sculpture—might mean the islanders burned the idols there after the missionaries arrived.

In 1995 paleontologist David Steadman of the New York State Museum reported on research he and other scientists had done on birds of several Pacific islands, including Easter Island. By analyzing discarded food bones, they found that the early Easter Islanders ate both seabirds and land birds. Steadman and the others also determined that of the twenty-five species of seabirds once found on the island, eight to ten no longer breed on the island, and thirteen to sixteen no longer breed even on any of its offshore islets. Among the extinct land birds are herons, owls, and certain kinds of parrots and rails.

Ecologists, scientists who study the relationships between organisms and their environment, are looking at the ways the early islanders impacted their local landscape and the consequences of their actions. The ecologists believe that by using their natural resources unwisely, the early islanders destroyed habitats for birds, ruined the soil, depleted the forest, and contaminated the water supply. As a result, the island no longer could support its population. The ecologists see what occurred on Rapa Nui as an object lesson for people in other parts of the world.

Mysteries Remain

Despite the many things scientists and scholars have learned, one of the island's most famous puzzles has not yet been solved: How did the islanders manage to move the huge carved statues from the quarry, transport them several miles across the island, and raise them onto platforms?

A few highly trained linguists and classics scholars are still trying to decipher the messages on the rongorongo tablets. So far, no one has succeeded in figuring out what the hieroglyphs mean.

Although recent studies have concluded that the island was densely wooded only a few hundred years before the first outsiders arrived, the haunting question still remains: How, in such a short time, could the fertile, forested island have become a near wasteland with no trees? Was it the result of human actions? Pests? A natural disaster—disease, a cyclone, a sudden climate change, or a long drought?

Although most modern-day scholars reject the theory that there was a battle between the long ears and the short ears at Poike Ditch, they still wonder why the people dug this two-mile-long stretch of trenches that separates the eastern tip of land from the rest of the island. Was it an early effort at irrigation? Was it to create a canal for water to use on crops? They also want to know more about the pukao, the large cylinders atop the heads of some statues. What was their purpose? Why did only certain statues have them?

Scientists and scholars also want to know more about what the settlements of the early islanders were like and what the relationship was between these settlements and the ahu and moai. With every search, they find one or two more pieces of the puzzle. Although all of the pieces will probably never be found, a few more might be. And so the rediscovery of this remarkable island continues.

HISTORIANS AND PREHISTORIANS

Dictionaries define history as a narrative of past events arranged in order of time—in other words, history is a record of what happened to people and when. The person who compiles that record is a historian.

A prehistorian, on the other hand, is a person who studies the remains, customs, and conditions of prehistoric times—the period before written or recorded history. While historians have ships' logs, newspapers, letters, and books to inform them about Easter Island after its discovery by a Dutch sea captain in 1722, the historians can only speculate about the island's fascinating prehistory. For the early islanders had no written language—only a few rongorongo tablets with carved hieroglyphs no one has been able to translate. There are no messages inscribed on monuments or other written records that tell historians when the first settlers arrived, how they established a society and a religion, how they carved and transported those giant statues—and why they suddenly destroyed everything they had created.

To understand this part of the island's history, the world depends on prehistorians to find out what happened and when. Prehistorians try to do this with the help of experts such as anthropologists (who study people's physical characteristics and culture), archaeologists (who study the human past through its material remains), palynologists (who analyze fossil pollen in order to reconstruct past vegetation and climates), and ethnographers (who study living cultures).

When historians do research, they use both secondary sources of information, such as books and articles by other historians, and primary sources. Serious historians try to use as many primary sources as they can find. Primary sources—the "raw material of history"—include original diaries, official legal documents, and eyewitness accounts. But in the case of Easter Island, there were no primary or secondary sources prior to 1722. And even long after the first Europeans arrived, much of what was known was sketchy, since most of the observers were not trained scientists or scholars. Some of the people—such as those who merely sailed by and looked at the island through a telescope and then reported on what they thought they had seen—gave superficial or inaccurate accounts.

Besides written records or evidence from an archaeological dig, there is a third source of information about Easter Island history. In the late 1800s and early 1900s, researchers such as Wilhelm Geiseler and Katherine Routledge heard songs, stories, and chants that—the people claimed—revealed the island's history back to the time the legendary Hotu Matu`a first arrived. But nobody knows how much truth—if any—there is in this tradition of oral history.

Although it is popular to talk about the mysteries of Easter Island, in truth there are many unknowns but no mysteries. No one is sure where the original islanders came from, but there are many possible places. It is not known exactly how the giant statues were moved or erected, but again there are many ways it could have been done. And although no one knows why the statues were destroyed, there are several logical explanations. With practically no likelihood of discovering the complete truth, some of these "unknowns" may never be resolved.

NOTES

14–15   Alfred Métraux, *Ethnology of Easter Island*, Bulletin 160. (1940; reprint. Honolulu, HI: Bernice P. Bishop Museum, 1971), pp. 55–65.

22   Much later, in the 1800s, researchers learned that Makemake (pronounced MAHK-ee MAHK-ee) was the name of the man-god of the birdman cult.

23   Bolton G. Corney, *The Voyage of Captain Don Felipe González* (Cambridge, England: Hakluyt Society, 1908).

30   Some years later, in 1826, parts of what must have been the wreckage of the two French ships were found near the Solomon Islands in the South Pacific.

31   John Dos Passos, *Easter Island: Island of Enigmas* (Garden City, NY: Doubleday & Company, Inc., 1971), pp. 64–65.

44   Métraux, *Ethnology of Easter Island*, p. 45.

45   Supposedly, the new name came from Polynesians in Peru who met Easter Islanders working there as slaves. Modern-day islanders call themselves and their traditional language Rapanui.

54   Wilhelm Geiseler, *Easter Island Report, an 1880s Anthropological Account*, translated by William S. Ayres and Gabriella Ayres (Honolulu, HI: University of Hawaii Social Science Research Institute, 1995), p. 80.

58   William J. Thomson, *Te Pito te Henua: or Easter Island* (Washington, DC: Government Printing Office, 1891), p. 484.

65   Katherine Routledge, *The Mystery of Easter Island* (London: Sifton, Praed & Co., Ltd., 1919), p. 172.

69   Ibid., p. 212.

69   Ibid.

72   Alfred Métraux, *Easter Island: A Stone-Age Civilization of the Pacific* (London: André Deutsch Ltd., 1957), p. 17.

73   Some researchers think she was Tepano's grandmother rather than his mother.

75   Métraux, *Ethnology of Easter Island*, p. 4.

77   Métraux, *Easter Island*, p. 59.

80   Father Sebastian Englert, *Island at the Center of the World: New Light on Easter Island* (New York: Charles Scribner's Sons, 1970), p. 152.

81   Thor Heyerdahl, *Aku-Aku, The Secret of Easter Island* (London: George Allen & Unwin Ltd., 1958), p. 37.

93   Jo Anne Van Tilburg, *Easter Island* (Washington, D.C.: Smithsonian Institution Press, 1994), p. 148.

93   Paul Bahn and John Flenley, *Easter Island, Earth Island* (London: Thames and Hudson, 1992), p. 152.

94   Ibid., p. 157.

95   Ibid., p. 92, and Routledge, p. 228.

95   Van Tilburg, p. 107.

98   J. B. Clegg, E. Hagelberg, S. Quevedo, and D. Turbon, "DNA from Ancient Easter Islanders (DNA from Human Bones from Easter Island near Chile)," *Nature*, May 5, 1994, pp. 25–26.

98   Métraux, *Easter Island*, p. 102.

99   Heyerdahl, p. 73.

99   Bahn and Flenley, p. 171.

99   Van Tilburg, p. 110.

100 Arne Skjølsvold, ed., *Archaeological Investigations at Anakena, Easter Island* (Oslo: The Kon-Tiki Museum Occasional Papers, vol. 3, 1994), p. 200.

100 David Steadman, "Prehistoric Extinctions of Pacific Island Birds: Biodiversity Meets Zoo Archaeology," *Science*, February 24, 1995, pp. 1123–1129.

SOURCES OF INFORMATION

I began my library research on Easter Island by reading Jo Anne Van Tilburg's *Easter Island* (Washington, DC: Smithsonian Institution Press, 1994), a large book that provides an excellent review of island history and a long and detailed report on work there by Van Tilburg and her fellow archaeologists. In their much smaller book, *Easter Island: Mystery of the Stone Giants* (New York: Harry N. Abrams, 1995), Catherine and Michel Orliac give a brief overview of the island and its history. Another excellent survey of Easter Island with both a historical and a present-day perspective is Grant McCall's *Rapanui: Tradition and Survival on Easter Island* (Honolulu, HI: University of Hawaii Press, 1994).

I also read several books by earlier visitors to the island. In his 1940 monograph *Ethnology of Easter Island* (reprint, Honolulu, HI: Bernice P. Bishop Museum, 1971), Alfred Métraux described parts of the 1934–1935 French–Belgian expedition. But Métraux's longer *Easter Island: A Stone-Age Civilization of the Pacific* (London: André Deutsch Ltd., 1957) is a classic, with much more interesting and useful information. I also enjoyed Katherine Routledge's *The Mystery of Easter Island* (London: Sifton, Praed and Co., Ltd., 1919), a delightful account of her experiences during her 1915–1916 expedition, and Thor Heyerdahl's popular *Aku-Aku, The Secret of Easter Island* (New York: George Allen & Unwin, Ltd., 1958), which tells of his 1955–1956 expedition to the island.

In *Easter Island: Land of Mysteries* (New York: Rinehart & Winston, 1976), author Peggy Mann interweaves island history with details from her visit to the island. John Dos Passos visited Easter Island a few years earlier. In *Easter Island: Island of Enigmas* (Garden City, NY: Doubleday, 1971), Dos Passos includes reprints of logs, reports, and journals of early visitors—useful if you are unable to track down the originals. Fortunately, in the reading room of the Royal Geographical Society in London, I was able to read some of those originals. The books included Bolton G. Corney's *The Voyage of Captain Don Felipe González in the Ship of the Line San Lorenzo with the Frigate Santa Rosalia in Company, to Easter Island in 1770–71; Preceded by an Extract from Mynheer Jacob Roggeveen's Official Log of his Discovery of and Visit to Easter Island in 1722* (Cambridge, England: Hakluyt Society, 1908), James Cook's *A Voyage Towards the South Pole and Round the World Performed in His Majesty's Ships, The Resolution and Adventure, in the years 1772–75, vol. 2* (London: W. Strahan & T. Cadell, 1777), and Alexander Dalrymple's *An Historical Collection of the Several Voyages and Discoveries in the South Pacific Ocean, vol. 1* (London: J. Nourse, T. Payne, & P. Elmsly, 1770).

I was able to order several other hard-to-find books through the interlibrary loan program. These included Father Sebastian Englert's *Island at the Center of the World: New Light on Easter Island* (New York: Charles Scribner's Sons, 1970) with legends and stories Father Sebastian learned from the islanders; the report of William J. Thomson, *Te Pito te Henua: or Easter Island,* (Washington, DC: Government Printing Office, 1891); and Geiseler's *Easter Island Report, an 1880s Anthropological Account,* (Honolulu, HI: University of Hawaii Social Science Research Institute, 1995), translated by William S. Ayres and Gabriella Ayres.

To find out how archaeologists do their job, I read the very readable *Archaeology: Theories, Methods & Practice* (New York: Thames & Hudson, 1991) by Colin Renfrew and Paul Bahn. Bahn is also the author, with John Flenley, of *Easter Island, Earth Island* (New York: Thames & Hudson, 1992), a report on what historians and prehistorians have learned about this tiny island and a suggestion that the abandoned statues might be "a timely warning for us all, as guardians of our own fragile natural world—Earth Island."

To learn more about rock art and present-day travel to Easter Island, I read Georgia Lee's *An Uncommon Guide to Easter Island: Exploring Archaeological Mysteries of Rapa Nui* (Arroyo Grande, CA: International Resources, 1990). And in Steven Fischer's *Rongorongo* (Oxford, England: Clarendon, 1997), I learned about the history of the mysterious rongorongo tablets and the ongoing search for their meaning.

Magazines and journals often provided useful information, too. Among the articles I discovered were William Mulloy's "Easter Island" *(Natural History* 76, No. 10, 1967) and David Steadman's "Prehistoric Extinctions of Pacific Island Birds: Biodiversity Meets Zoo Archaeology" *(Science,* February 24, 1995).

If you decide to become a historian—or even act like one and do historical research—a good way to begin is to look up the subject you are researching in an encyclopedia. After you read the entry, check for a bibliography at the end. It will list books and documents the author of the entry used to get information. You may want to read these books, too. You can find bibliographies in other nonfiction books, too. And if you read those books, you will find that usually they, too, contain bibliographies. Eventually you will find that books you have already read are being cited, so you can see that various writers draw on one another as sources—and facts as well as fallacies can be repeated throughout the references.

INDEX

About the Author: Kathy Pelta has written short stories, mysteries, and nonfiction for young readers, including the highly acclaimed *Discovering Christopher Columbus*, published by the Lerner Publishing Group in 1991. She has also written *Bridging the Golden Gate*, which in 1987 received the Honorable Mention in the Children's Science Book Award Program of the New York Academy of Sciences. *Rediscovering Easter Island* is her twenty-first book. Pelta and her husband live on a peninsula on the coast of Maine.

Photo Acknowledgments: © Wolfgang Kaehler, pp. 2-3, 17, 27, 30, 32, 38, 44 (right), 52, 54, 72, 97; Archive Photos: pp. 6, 12, 24, 59, (Camera Press, Ltd.) p. 81; © Daniel Monconduit/Liaison Agency, Inc., p. 10; North Wind Picture Archives, p. 13; Bishop Museum: pp. 20, 34, 35, 44 (left and center), 53, 71, (Dr. Alfred Métraux) pp. 66, 90; Biblioteca Central de la Diputacion de Barcelona. Courtesy Francisco Mellen-Blanco, p. 23; © Stock Montage, p. 29; © Royal Geographical Society, pp. 46, 62, 65, 68, 70, 76, 79; Corbis: (© Leonard de Selva) p. 48, (© The Mariners' Museum) p. 57, (© James L. Amos) pp. 94, 99; National Anthropological Archives, Smithsonian Institution, #81-2890, p. 50; Peter Arnold, Inc.: (© James L. Amos) pp. 55, 60, 74, 88, 92, 96, (© Fred Bruemmer) p. 58; From *Mystery of Easter Island* by Katherine Routledge, p. 64; The Kon-Tiki Museum, Oslo, Norway, pp. 85, 87; © Jose Nuñez, p. 89.

Front cover, © James L. Amos/Peter Arnold, Inc. (top); © Wolfgang Kaehler (bottom); back cover, © Wolfgang Kaehler.